If you want to know your future...
Learn to read your hands.

Etched in your palms are clues to your character, goals, destiny. Once you understand these messages, you can fulfill all your potential for a richer and fuller life.

A famed occultist will teach you what the hand reveals about personality, problems, prospects. Within hours, you'll be able to answer questions about your and your friends' careers, chances for success in marriage, love, children, health, travel —and more! There are fascinating sections on palmistry as influenced by the stars, numbers and other mystic symbols. You'll discover what the hand has to say about the cosmic meaning of existence and the true path to spiritual development. Two actual palms are read to show you how it's really done.

Learn these secrets of palmistry easily, quickly. You'll delight and profit one and all with your uncanny gift for "seeing into the future."

YOUR FATE IS IN YOUR HANDS!

the complete book of PALMISTRY

BY JOYCE WILSON

BANTAM BOOKS

TORONTO · NEW YORK · LONDON · SYDNEY · AUCKLAND

THE COMPLETE BOOK OF PALMISTRY

A Bantam Book / published by arrangement with Workman Publishing Company, Inc.

PRINTING HISTORY

Bantam edition / March 1971

2nd printing ... December 1972	8th printing .... June 1979
3rd printing ... September 1973	9th printing .. November 1980
4th printing ...... August 1974	10th printing .... January 1982
5th printing ...... August 1975	11th printing ... February 1982
6th printing ...... August 1976	12th printing .. December 1983
7th printing ...... March 1978	13th printing .. September 1985

ISBN 0-553-25595-9

Published simultaneously in the United States and Canada

Bantam Books are published by Bantam Books, Inc. Its trademark, consisting of the words "Bantam Books" and the portrayal of a rooster, is Registered in U.S. Patent and Trademark Office and in other countries. Marca Registrada. Bantam Books, Inc., 666 Fifth Avenue, New York, New York 10103.

PRINTED IN THE UNITED STATES OF AMERICA

O   22   21   20   19   18   17   16   15   14   13

CONTENTS

INTRODUCTION:
WHAT IS PALMISTRY?

What is palmistry? Popularly, it is "fortune-telling" by means of the lines of the palm. Will I get married? And when? How many times? How many children will I have? Will I travel? Be rich? Famous? Succeed at my job? Stay healthy? Live a long time?

These are questions we're all interested in — and should be. This is life. We all look to the future — and there it is, right in your hand.

But palmistry is more than that. It is one of the esoteric, or occult, sciences, older than recorded time, its origin lost. By means of it, ancient kings were warned of sudden death and disastrous conquest. Spiritual leaders (the Buddha himself) were recognized. Heroes were apprised of victory in battle. Miscreants were advised of hanging or beheading, to flee their enemies or to mend their ways.

The real value of palmistry is to help you understand your own destiny — in the words of the oracle to "know yourself." To understand your potentials and limitations, your talents and restrictions, to help you develop the whole of your many-sided nature. You may say "I am what I am," but to *become* what you are, you need to *know* what you are.

A study of the hand tells much about seven areas of human activity:

• The physical body — health, vitality, strength.
• The emotional nature — love potential, sexuality, marriage.
• The will and individuality — "your own thing."

- Success in business and other enterprises.
- Talent and imagination, creativity.
- Fame or public approval.
- Self-fulfillment—travel, life experience, spiritual development.

Once you understand, through palmistry, your capacities in these various areas, you are better able to fulfill your destiny, perhaps to control it—maybe even to change it for the better.

Can you change your fate? Predestination and free will are not really incompatible—but for most mentalities they seem to be, and you will only waste time if you argue the point. True, our destiny is in our hand, but how we react to events is within our control. A blow on the head is a blow on the head—but a stoic will accept it; a fighter will turn and fight; a masochist will enjoy it; an amnesiac might recover his memory as a result of it; another man might lose his memory because of it; an optimist will say, "How lucky it is I am wearing my wig, or it might have been worse."

A study of palmistry can help make us more optimistic about our destiny and thus help us control our reactions to what fate brings us—and as we well know from our childhood stories, ugly fate can be changed by a kiss into a princely presence. The way we meet our fate has much to do with how it affects us.

In palmistry, the left hand is said to show the destiny we are born with; the right hand shows how this destiny is used. A great difference in the two hands shows that a force other than fate has been at work in the life—call it what you like. True, people warned of illness, accident, or reversals of fortune are often powerless to avoid them—a pedestrian dodges a truck in order to be hit by a falling brick. But we can be helped by warnings if we realize the change must be inside us—in attitudes, courage, willingness to enjoy experience. We change our destiny when we change ourselves.

8

How can you use palmistry? Apart from the fascinating purpose of getting new insight into yourself and into those of your friends who let you look into their palm, palmistry can be used as a pleasant party pastime — a way to get yourself stage center and also to contribute to others' enjoyment. It is also helpful in understanding strangers, for as you study hands, even from a distance, you begin to get insight into the person you are dealing with — a prospective employer or employee, a businessman with whom you must work, a possible companion. Perhaps the easiest way to establish intimacy with another — and to find out if you really want to know him (her) better — is to say: "Let me look at your hand." But from there on, you'd better know what you are doing, because the respect and affection of the other may turn upon your tact, courtesy, insight, and awareness of what the life goals of this individual may be.

Why the hand? First, because it is one of our most human features. It is closely connected with the brain and eye, and these three organs working together have created man as a distinctive creature. The length of our fingers and our mobile thumb have made it possible for us to be toolmakers — and helped develop the brain. Much of the quality of the mentality is shown in the hand. A weak, short, undeveloped thumb is, for example, often found in the mentally retarded.

In caves where prehistoric art has been preserved, one of the most interesting and curious recurrences is the imprint of a hand on the cave wall. So universal is this symbolism that one can only guess that the hand in primitive culture was the image, or portrait, of the man. His sign.

In ancient religious symbolism the hand of God, often shown issuing from a cloud, represented the Divine Will. In astrology, the two hands represent the higher elements — fire and air; the feet, the lower elements — earth and water.

Man is believed to have learned to count — one, two — on his hands; then up to ten on his fingers.

The left hand was once considered to belong to the spiritual nature (the dark side) and the right hand to the active nature (light). Later, through a mistaken association of dark with evil, the left hand became identified with the dark forces — our word sinister originally meant simply "left." Today, all but about five percent of our population is right-handed, though it is believed that people were originally about equally divided among right- and left-handers. Traditionally, the gypsies, who kept palmistry and card-reading alive in the Western world for many generations, read the left hand. Perhaps because it represents the esoteric, or occult, side of the individual, perhaps because it is "nearer the heart."

The handshake has long been the symbol of friendship among men; the raised hand of the priest gives the blessing; the union of hands is the symbol of marriage; in taking an oath we raise the right hand.

The hand has also been used for secret languages — areas on the fingers indicating the various letters of the alphabet. In the presently used sign language, the hand is the means by which the deaf hear and the mute speak.

In occultism, man represents the microcosm (little world) of the universe (macrocosm). He is the five-pointed star — the head, two arms, and the legs representing the five points. The hand is likewise said to be the man in microcosm — the thumb and four fingers being the five points. So it should not seem strange that, when one looks into the palm, one sees the whole life in miniature.

In this book I have tried to present, as simply and clearly as possible, the keys to the understanding of the age-old science of palmistry. It is not my purpose to teach you how to become a professional palm-reader (for that would take many years of devoted application to the occult arts.) My intention is, rather, to help you master — step-by-step, the elements of hand-reading, so that you can begin to read and interpret what is revealed therein about the character and future prospects of yourself and your friends.

By reading these pages, and applying your new knowledge to actual palm-readings, you will gradually learn how to analyze not only the lines of the palm but of the entire hand as a whole. With more experience, you will be able to observe — and evaluate — the shape and size of the fingers and hands, and such qualities as color, firmness, gestures, flexibility, warmth, and so forth. For all of these delineations are highly significant in determining the personality, potential, traits and destiny of the subject whose hand is being read.

I have also included a concise section on the relationship of astrology to palmistry, since many of the lines and markings of the hand are named for planets, and are influenced by the rulership of these planets. Those interested in planetary numbers — as clues to the personality and destiny of the subject — may benefit from my brief discussion of palmistry and numerology.

As you delve more deeply, you will begin to realize that the hand is the mirror of our past and future lives as well as of our present existence. In its lines and mounts can be found the true path of one's spiritual development.

My explanation of esoteric palmistry is intended to provide disciples and students alike with the needed knowledge in this profound phase of palmistry. I sincerely hope that this will help them to discover in the message of the hand how they can best fulfill their Divine Destiny that comes from living in accordance with the Cosmic Will.

— Joyce Wilson

1 / HOW TO READ A PALM

What we love about raccoons and what makes us nervous about apes is the *humanness* of their hands. They use theirs the way we do ours. What is charming in the little unlike-a-person raccoon is unnerving in the very-like-us gorilla or orangutan. We think of our hands as our SELF and want to reserve them for our own species.

What makes the human hand so human? It is the length of the fingers in proportion to the palm and the length and mobility of the thumb. It should come as no surprise to us—but it does—that the shape, size, and even the lines on the hand are genetically determined. That is, the genes that give you your other physical characteristics—the color of eyes, texture of hair, complexion, body shape, and so forth—have *predestined*, so to speak, the lines you now look upon in your hand...have predetermined the knottiness of your knuckles and the shape of your fingernails, both of which we shall be considering in delineating character from the hands. Disease may of course intervene—arthritis can knot a knuckle; thyroid malfunction or other disorders can afflict the fingernails. But what we look at in the hand is destiny as revealed by inherited human characteristics.

Medical men and women are in fact aware of many of the characteristic inherited defects as shown in the hand. A retarded child has the characteristic short thumb and palm print that reveal (or confirm) mental deficiency. And many other genetic disorders show up in the shape of hands and fingers and fingernails. The color of the palm and of the skin of the back of the hand are diagnostic clues. When you next visit a doctor, observe him as he shakes hands with you. He is observing your hand with a practiced eye while he makes this seemingly casual welcoming gesture.

Eventually you will find yourself doing a similar thing—making a careful routine examination of all hands you come in contact with for their soon-to-be-obvious characteristics.

You begin to read a hand long before its owner thrusts it out and says: "What's going to happen to me?" Your first clue is the handclasp. If you are interested in palmistry, you will discover that it is not only cordial but also informative to clasp hands with anyone to whom you are introduced. Often at this first contact you can tell whether or not you might want to read this particular hand.

• Observation is your second step. Watch how a person uses his hands. Sometimes the hands lie flatly on the thighs or chair arms or are quietly clasped in the lap for long periods; others use their hands constantly, and the hands fly about like birds during a conversation; in still other individuals, the hands are used for deliberate affirmative gestures only—a kind of forceful dramatic play; others make painful nervous gestures; there are people who hide their hands, stuffing them into pockets or even sitting on them! This use of the hands is an important lead into the character.

• Hand shape and size, the relative smoothness or knottiness of the fingers, are also readable across a room. Make it a habit, while you are learning, of evaluating the hand type of every individual you have a chance to observe. It is only with this kind of experience that you can come to distinguish the various kinds of hands unerringly.

• Usually, when a person wants you to read his palm, he thrusts it out to you palm up. It is courteous to observe the palm that is offered and to make some comment at once—even if it is only "How interesting!" But usually it is best to say the first thing that comes into your mind about the hand, because this is often a kind of message that accompanies the first contact—a form of clairvoyance or insight that will reinforce your careful delineation of the hand. Then take the other hand and quickly compare them before you begin to analyze the hand as a whole.

• Be prepared at this point to note the hand that you do not want to read. It is inevitable that some hands will repel you. Other hands may show indications of mental derangement, violence, or perhaps sorcery. You should firmly refuse to read such hands and be ready with a comment that will nicely free you from the responsibility: "Oh, but you must want your secrets kept." "What an exciting life—you could tell me more interesting things than I can tell you." Or, decidedly: "Haven't we had enough of palmistry for one evening? What about some music?" Don't just defer the situation by saying you'll read the palm another time. If you don't mean to, don't say you will.

Actual reading of the palm should proceed in an orderly fashion. When we start to read a hand as a beginner, we look first to the lines. The lines of the hand, especially the major lines which we learn about first, are a little like the astrological sun sign. Everybody has one and nearly everyone knows what his sign is. So, in the palm we all have a life line, a head line, and usually a heart line—and the beginning palmist (or even the most uninformed person) is aware of these.

A great deal can actually be learned about a person from this very rudimentary knowledge. If, when you start reading a palm, you learn to recognize and to read the basic lines—life, heart, head—you are farther along than you can even guess. And you really can tell a lot about your subject from just these lines.

As you become more informed, you begin to understand more about the other lines—and to recognize them. You also begin to evaluate the hand and fingers in regard to their shape; the thumb in regard to its flexibility and form. In fact, as you become a much more sophisticated palm reader, you should begin to conduct your reading in reverse order. Let the person place his or her hands before you on a table top, palms down, so you can observe the shape of the hands and fingers and the knottiness or smoothness of the knuckles, the spread of the fingers, the relative size and spread of the thumb in relation to the hand as a whole.

- Then ask the person to turn the hands over so that you can see the palms and evaluate the color, the clarity of the lines, the relative hollowness of the palm, and the similarity and difference of the two palms.
- Usually the left hand is read first — and then the right hand is compared with it to confirm, strengthen, or modify the evidence of the left hand.
- Pick up the left hand and test it for flexibility — at the wrist, at the finger joints, at the thumb.
- Test it for spread of thumb from the fingers.
- Test the palm for firmness of flesh.
- Test the ball of the thumb for fullness and firmness.
- Test the right hand for the same points.

You thus know (or will with a little experience) the character and personality you are dealing with as revealed in the quality of the hands and then you can read the lines and areas of the hand in relation to this basic personality. Keep in mind then, that you should eventually do your delineations in the following order:

- Delineations based on hand-shape, flexibility, and color.
- Delineations based on finger length, shape, knuckles, and the balls of the fingers.
- Delineations based on the thumb, its flexibility, size and the firmness of the flesh at the ball of the thumb.
- Delineations based on the areas of the palm according to their firmness and the degree of development.
- Delineations based on the lines, starting with the life line, the head line, and the heart line in that order.
- Delineations based on the line of health, the line of fate, the line of fame.
- Delineations based on the lines of marriage, children, travel.
- Major markings — angle of luck, angle of generosity, magic M, mystic cross, battle cross, and so forth.
- Minor lines and markings.
- Be sure to save for the end something particularly

pleasant — good luck or good fortune promised soon. If nothing else, you can say for a strong-handed person: "You make your own luck." For a weak-handed person: "There'll always be someone to help you out."

Before you start to read the lines and areas of the left hand, gently caress the middle of the palm with your thumb or index finger. A basic artery of the hand flows under the ball of the thumb and there is also said to be a "psychic center" in the palm of the hand that, when stimulated, will aid you in communicating the things of importance that you see in the palm. True, events of the life — important journeys, changes in status, danger, marriage, and so forth — and the age at which they are likely to occur can be read in the lines of the palm. But when a palmist sees the color of your future mate's hair and eyes and church at which you are to be married, her visualization is being arrived at by clairvoyance in association with the events indicated by the lines. Professional palmists are somewhat mediumistic and "see" events this way. As you pursue palmistry, you will find your own ESP sharpened — and will begin to "read between the lines," so to speak, perhaps even to see future events (clairvoyance) or to hear (clairaudience) things happen.

Although you will want to observe everything about the hand to help your reading, it isn't necessary to tell the individual everything step by step. This is not to say you shouldn't "tell it as it is," but that there often are contradictions that you should resolve in your own mind and then come up with the dominant indication: "You have a tendency to let people walk all over you, but when something really matters, they'll find you have a bar of steel inside." "You have a potential for the arts that you've never developed. Maybe you should pay a little attention to music and painting along with making money."

• When it comes to potential disasters, speak with care. Indication of a major sickness at a certain point in life can be handled this way: "Your health is generally good, but a problem develops about age 45. Better watch things a little after age 40." For a serious accident: "You're inclined to be a bit of a daredevil—and you need to watch that accident hazard about age 30. Start driving a little more carefully now." Most people today are interested in love, money, success, travel—and care less about health and life expectancy than they used to when life was more precarious. As a beginner, it is wise to confine your reading to the four high-interest areas rather than to foretell disasters, which take some experience to define.

• If you run into a confusing hand, it is wise to ask what questions the person wants answered: "There's so much in your hand—what particularly do you want to know about?" Then concentrate on answering the questions. A storehouse of tactful remarks is part of your preparation for palm-reading. Always call attention to potential good fortune when you see it in the hand.

The first palm to read is your own, first the left and then the right. Theoretically, the left hand shows your destiny; the right, how your own will and environment have modified this destiny. If you have trouble identifying the lines, it will help to outline them with a soft lead pencil or with a ballpoint pen with washout ink.

Proceed to inspection of the palms of family and friends. It helps educate you to be able to compare what the hand indicates to you with what you actually know of a person and his or her life. But be prepared for some surprises. Often we overevaluate or underestimate those near to us.

When you go on to read the palms of comparative strangers—people at parties or those working with you—you will soon become aware how individual and different hands can be. We all have individual palm prints. If palmistry does nothing else for you, it will impress upon you how various and multifaceted is the world of men and women—how rich each of us is in our own dreams, talents, and adventures.

2 / THE LINES

When we read a hand, we start with the shape of the hand, its flexibility, and the nature of the thumb. Each type of hand — there are five basic ones: the square, the pointed, the cone-shaped, the spade-shaped, and the mixed, as we shall describe them later — has its own characteristic types of lines and the meaning of the lines must be related to the hand type. But in learning to read the map of the hand, it is better and easier to start with a study of the lines themselves, to learn to recognize them in their many variations, and then to relate them to the various areas of the palm and to the fingers and thumb. This method has proved most effective with students.

Although every palm is different, each has certain identifiable lines that relate to a particular phase of the life of its owner. The major lines are:

- The life line — vitality and longevity.
- The head line — strength of intellect and mental set.
- The heart line — emotional set.

Secondary lines may or may not appear on the hand:
- The health line — physical strength and material gain.
- The line of fate — what destiny delivers to you.
- The line of fame — success and public image.

Minor lines — though they may not seem so to you — are found in most hands:
- Lines of marriage and children.
- Lines of travel.

- Money lines.
- Lines of opposition—just that.
- Line of intuition—gives insight.
- Lines of influence—predictors of events.
- Family lines—show how your family influences you in present, past, future.
- Sister lines—these can accompany any of the major or minor lines and reinforce the meaning of the line.

THE LINES
(illustrated)

1. LIFE
2. HEAD
3. HEART
4. HEALTH
5. FATE
6. FAME
7. MARRIAGE
8. CHILDREN
9. MONEY
10. SEX
11. SPIRIT
12. TRAVEL
13. LUCK

- Thumb chain — obstinacy.

There are also certain lines that have special significance when found on the hand:
- The girdle of Venus — sexual success.
- The ring of Solomon — spiritual destiny.
- The ring of Saturn — restrictions.
- Bracelets — good luck.

Very tiny lines form configurations that have their own special meanings, depending on where they fall and the shape they take. These are usually in the form of:

- Series
- Crosses
- Stars
- Triangles
- Squares
- Circles
- Islands
- Chance lines
- Worry lines.

The major lines mark off the palm into certain important areas. The life line marks off the mount of Venus (base of the thumb). Between the life line and the head line lies the great triangle. The size of this triangle is significant. Between the head line and the heart line lies the quadrangle, and the breadth of this area has meaning, as you shall see.

Above the heart line lie the mounts of various planets — elevated areas below the individual fingers; other mounts lie on the sides of the palm, the heel of the hand, and on the thumb. These mounts have certain characteristics, and lines that point toward one or another of them take on special meaning, depending on the character of the line and the mount.

Being able to recognize the lines is the first step. Once they are identified, it is necessary to evaluate their length, quality, depth, color — and to interpret the special markings on the lines that show events in the life and the time at which they take place.

Although it may sound formidable to start with, it will not be difficult if the lines are taken one at a time and the variations recognized.

We start with the basic line of the palm — the life line.

SPECIAL MARKINGS, MOUNTS AND AREAS
(illustrated)

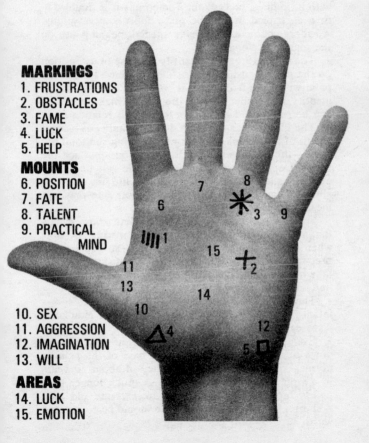

MARKINGS
1. FRUSTRATIONS
2. OBSTACLES
3. FAME
4. LUCK
5. HELP

MOUNTS
6. POSITION
7. FATE
8. TALENT
9. PRACTICAL MIND
10. SEX
11. AGGRESSION
12. IMAGINATION
13. WILL

AREAS
14. LUCK
15. EMOTION

THE LIFE LINE

The life line is one line you'll always find on the palm. It begins on the side of the palm between the thumb and index finger and heads down the middle of the palm along the base of the thumb. Sometimes it goes all the way around the base of the thumb. Usually, but not always, it is distinct. Sometimes it is deeply marked. Sometimes it is thin and wavery, chained, crisscrossed with little lines, or broken. Sometimes it is doubled—or even tripled. It can be quite short—or very long. All these characteristics have special meaning—as do the markings along it.

The life line is easy to identify because of its position on the palm—pushing the extended thumb toward the palm will make it clearer. It serves as a guide to the identity of the other lines on the palm, which sometimes can be recognized exactly only by their relation to it.

The life line has much to do with vitality as well as length of life. Think of it as representing the total life force—the effectiveness with which you approach the world. Depth and strength in this line can be as significant as length. An extremely long life line does not always mean a long life; a fairly short line may not mean an early death.

Special markings along the life line show events that affect the life force for better or worse. To know when in life these events take place—so you can be prepared for them and perhaps ease misfortunes and take better advantage of good periods—divide the life line into time zones this way:

• The start of the line at the side of the palm shows infancy; irregularities here show the usual childhood diseases.

• Evaluate the life expectancy. A line that swoops down to about an inch above the base of the palm is normal—it shows a life expectancy of about 70 years in a woman, 60 to 65 in men. A much longer line, unless broken, shows survival to extreme old age. A shorter but strong and deep line should be considered worth survival past middle age.

THE LIFE LINE
(illustrated)

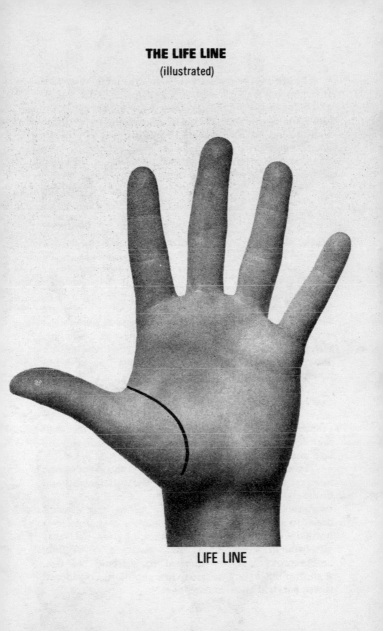

LIFE LINE

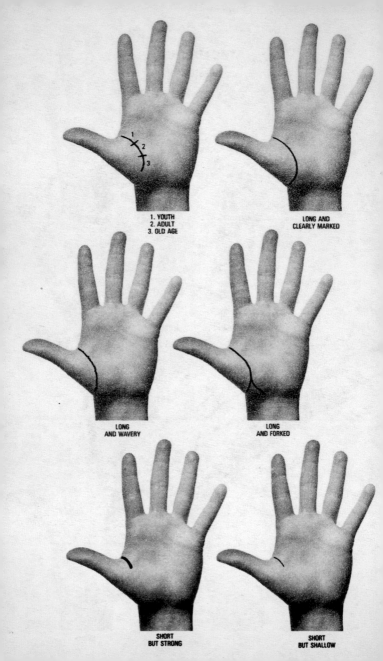

1. YOUTH
2. ADULT
3. OLD AGE

LONG AND
CLEARLY MARKED

LONG
AND WAVERY

LONG
AND FORKED

SHORT
BUT STRONG

SHORT
BUT SHALLOW

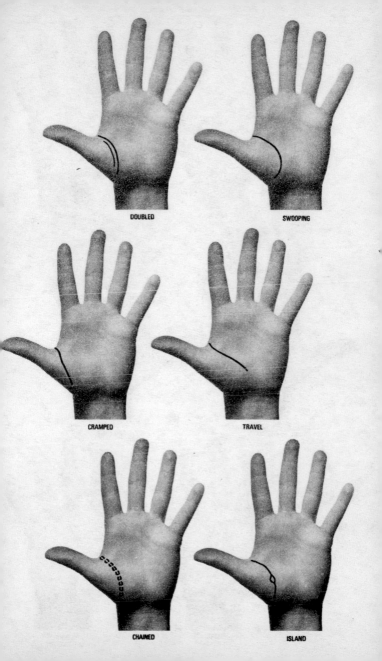

DOUBLED

SWOOPING

CRAMPED

TRAVEL

CHAINED

ISLAND

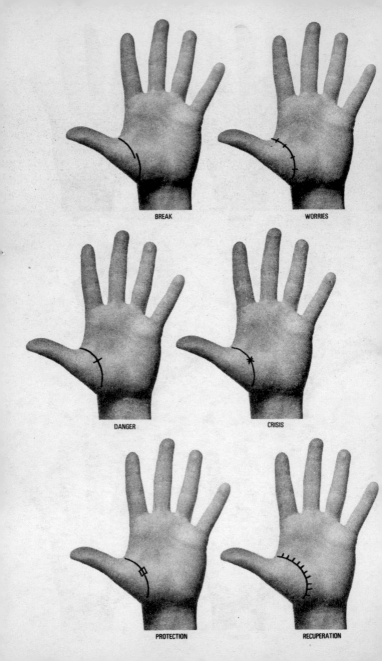

BREAK

WORRIES

DANGER

CRISIS

PROTECTION

RECUPERATION

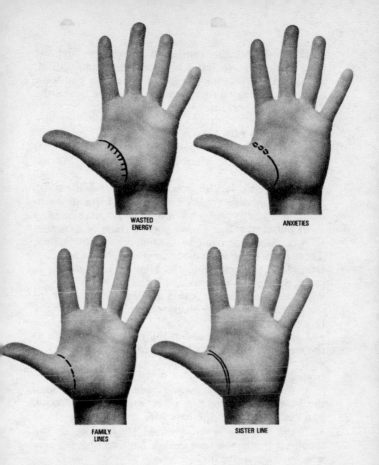

WASTED
ENERGY

ANXIETIES

FAMILY
LINES

SISTER LINE

• Divide the line into thirds and consider the first one third of the line to indicate youth; the middle third, adulthood; the last third, age. You can then pin down events according to their location along the line in the 20-to-25-year periods.

Evaluating the Life Line
• The life line is best if long and clearly marked. This shows good health, vitality, and reasonable life expectancy.
• The life line is also good when short and strong. Such a line shows vitality and drive and the ability to overcome health problems, if any. In a square hand, a short but strong line shows good chance of long life.
• A doubled — or tripled — life line is good for vitality. These extra lines are called vitality lines, and are considered a lucky marking. Doubling of any line shows protective forces at work.
• A long life line that is thin and wavering is poor for vitality and shows many changes as well as the possibility of variable health.
• Long and curving around the base of the thumb at the wrist, the line shows activity in age.
• If the line is short and shallow, it shows a life controlled by another's will.
• If the life line swoops in a wide semicircle around the base of the thumb, it gives strength, enthusiasm, and vastly improves the love life.
• If the life line is straight and clings close to the thumb, it limits the love nature and often shows one who lives a careful life.
• When the life line crosses the middle of the palm and reaches toward the base of the palm opposite the thumb, it means that travel will affect the life and there will be much imagination governing the life style.

Special Markings
• A chained life line or one much crosshatched is indicative of many health disturbances, perhaps of an emotional nature. Some of the allergy-afflicted have such life lines.

- An island means hospitalization or other closing in, for a time, of the energy or life situation, often because of a serious mishap.
- A break means an accident or serious illness or sudden change in the life situation.
- Little lines that cross the life line show worries.
- A cross means danger.
- A square gives protection at a time it is needed; sometimes it means that life from this point on improves.
- A star on the life line means a serious crisis.
- Little lines moving up from the life line show ability to recuperate; downward lines toward the thumb show a tendency to waste vitality.

These special markings show events that affect the health or life direction. Their position along the line shows the time in life the event will occur.

Because it embraces areas of life that involve the sex life, the will, the ego, the aggressive drive, the life line has a particular affinity not only with the physical vitality but also the magnetic animal nature, the aggressiveness and drive of the individual. Minor lines accompanying the life line are important:

- A doubled life line increases vitality. This sister line is often called the line of Mars (sexual vitality).
- A third series, or single line, that reinforces the life line is the line of family, which shows the influence of the family on the life of the individual. It can have branches that indicate money, fame, restriction, position, and so forth.
- A line at the base of the palm, originating within the life line and crossing it and other vertical lines of the lower palm and leading to the heel of the hand, is called the line of escape. It shows the vital forces escaping from the field of life into the realm of imagination.

A study of the life line alone can tell you much about the character and life of the person whose palm you are reading, but whatever you find there should be considered along with other lines in the palm and the configuration of the whole hand.

THE HEAD LINE

The head line — the line that shows the quality of the intellect and the mental set — is the second major line of the palm and one that, however short or weak, has to be there if you're going to make it. If there is only one crosswise line on the palm, this is the head line. If there are two — more or less parallel to each other — the head line is the lower of the two.

The head line begins on the side of the palm between the thumb and the index finger, just above the start of the life line (sometimes these lines are joined at the start) and is directed more or less horizontally across the middle of the hand.

Besides showing the mentality and power of the intellect, this line has much to do with attitudes toward life, philosophy, and the way you approach your problems. This line may run more or less straight across the hand or it may swing downward, along the curve of the life line, or it may head upward toward the base of the ring finger or the little finger. Sometimes it starts on the face of the palm just below the inside of the index finger.

Like the life line, it may be marked with chains, islands, stars, squares, crosses, breaks. The time in life when the events indicated by these markings occur can be judged by the distance along the line where the marking is found. Again, divide the line into three sections for youth, adulthood, and age, beginning with the start of the line on the inside of the palm below the index finger. If the head line and life line are joined at the start, use the start of the life line as the start of the head line.

Judging the Head Line

• If the head line and life line are joined at the start, it shows a strong sense of mind over body, a careful, even fearful, outlook, particularly in childhood.

• Separated at the start, it shows a love of adventure, one who greets the life experience with enthusiasm.

• If the line is long and deep and straight, running

THE HEAD LINE
(illustrated)

THE HEAD LINE

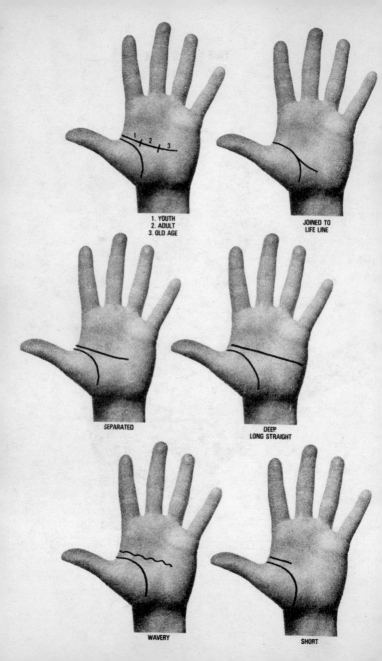

1. YOUTH
2. ADULT
3. OLD AGE

JOINED TO
LIFE LINE

SEPARATED

DEEP
LONG STRAIGHT

WAVERY

SHORT

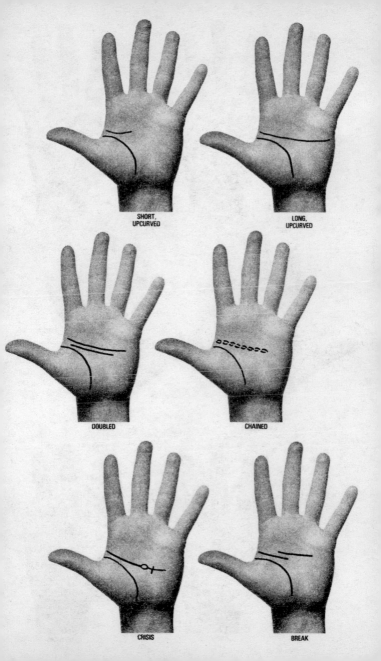

SHORT, UPCURVED

LONG, UPCURVED

DOUBLED

CHAINED

CRISIS

BREAK

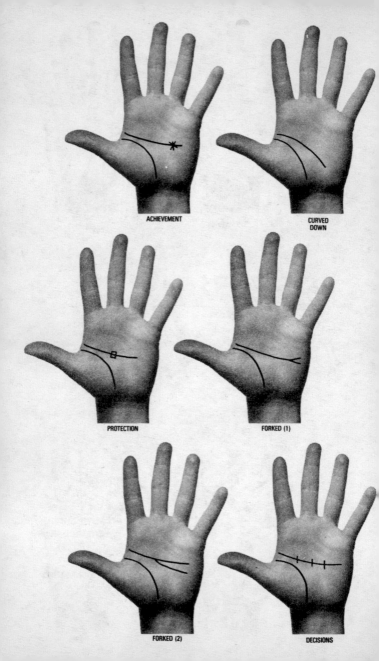

ACHIEVEMENT

CURVED DOWN

PROTECTION

FORKED (1)

FORKED (2)

DECISIONS

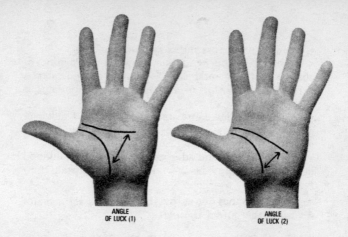

ANGLE
OF LUCK (1)

ANGLE
OF LUCK (2)

directly across the palm to the outer edge, it shows a
logical and direct mind, someone with a realistic and
outstanding intellect. The straighter the line, the more
realistic the thinking; the deeper the line, the better is
the memory.

• A light wavery line shows poor ability to concentrate
and lack of depth in thinking but not necessarily a lack
of intellectuality.
• Short, the line shows limited mental aims and a
tendency to "physical" thinking rather than reflection.
A short deep head line with a short deep life line is
often seen on the hands of men who have bulldozed
their way to success.
• Short and upcurved, the line means poor ability to
concentrate — a scatterbrain.
• A long line that heads upward sometimes shows a
retentive memory; sometimes it is the mark of the
collector.
• A long head line swooping down toward the heel of
the hand shows imaginative thinking — a creative mind.
• Doubled, the mental abilities are strengthened.

Special Markings
• A chained head line shows agitation and tensions in
the time of life where the chain appears.

- An island or cross indicates a mental crisis.
- A break in the head line shows some significant change in the mental set. Sometimes it indicates a nervous breakdown; overlapping and continuing, it shows recovery.
- A star signifies some outstanding mental achievement.
- A square shows guidance.
- Forked at the end, descent into second childhood in old age. Forked at the middle, an important new interest.
- Little lines that cut across the head line show major decisions that affect the life.

The Angle of Luck

Ideally, the head line is directed toward the opposite side of the palm while the life line curves back toward the base of the thumb. The wider the space between the end of the head line and the end of the life line, the better for you. This space is called "the angle of luck." If the space between these lines is narrow, good fortune is less than likely to fall into your hands; if the angle is wide, lucky you are.

THE HEART LINE

The heart line shows emotional attitudes — the ability to love and be loved and also the joys and frustrations that surround love relationships. It tells what you are like in love, what you look for in a mate. For most of us, it is the most interesting line in the hand.

The heart line is the upper of the two horizontal lines in the hand. It starts under the index finger or under the middle finger and runs across the palm to the outside of the palm below the little finger. Sometimes this line is missing. If there is only one horizontal line on the palm, it is the head line. We must treat such a palm as if the head line and the heart line were combined. The head will rule the heart. As a few minutes of conversation with the person who has this configuration will show you, emotional values play no part in his life; he will be reasonable to the point of becoming

THE HEART LINE
(illustrated)

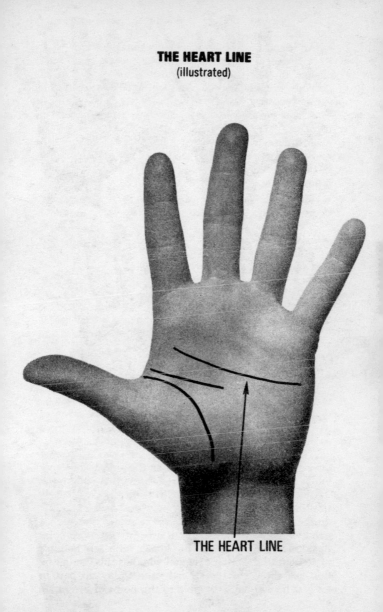

THE HEART LINE

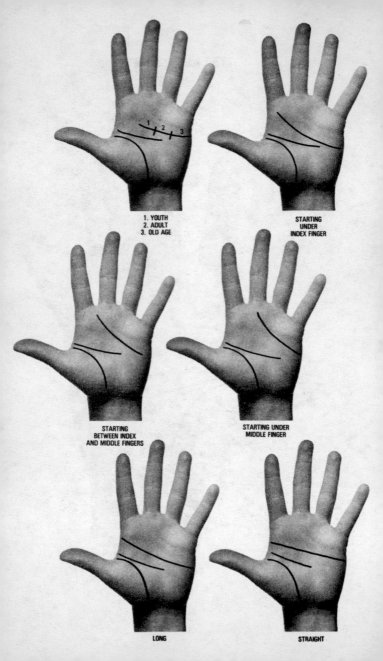

1. YOUTH
2. ADULT
3. OLD AGE

STARTING
UNDER
INDEX FINGER

STARTING
BETWEEN INDEX
AND MIDDLE FINGERS

STARTING UNDER
MIDDLE FINGER

LONG

STRAIGHT

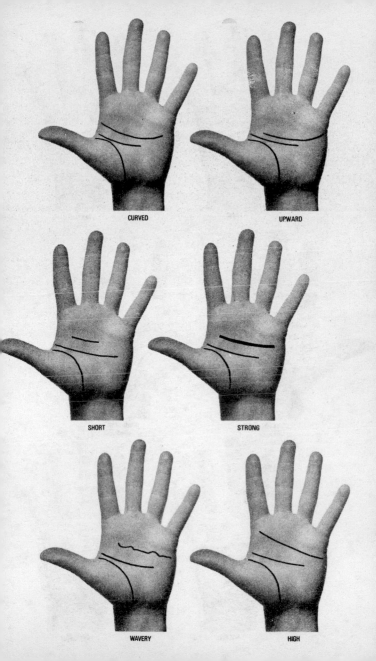

CURVED

UPWARD

SHORT

STRONG

WAVERY

HIGH

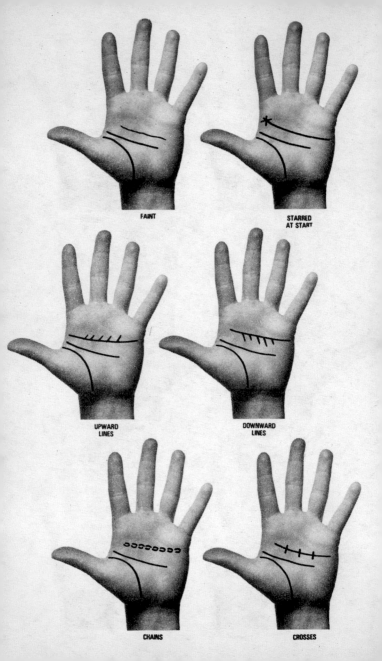

FAINT

STARRED AT START

UPWARD LINES

DOWNWARD LINES

CHAINS

CROSSES

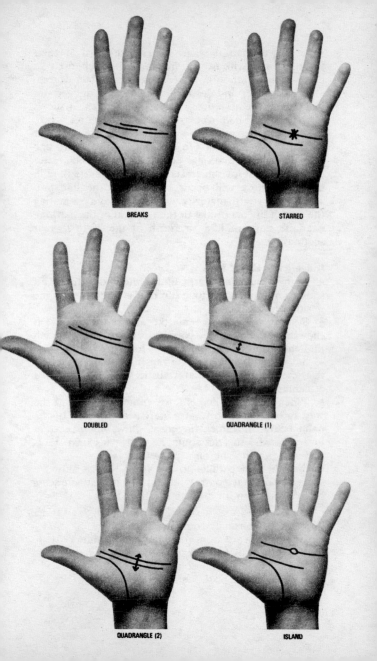

BREAKS

STARRED

DOUBLED

QUADRANGLE (1)

QUADRANGLE (2)

ISLAND

ridiculous in matters where others are ruled by their feelings — and will expect his mate and children to control their emotions to an unreasonable degree.

The stronger and deeper the heart line, the warmer and deeper the affections; wavery or broken, it shows fickleness and shallowness. Doubled, it denotes a protective influence over the emotional life. Like the other major lines — those of life and head — the heart line often has special markings pointing to emotional crises or to important love interests. Again, judge the time in life when those will occur by dividing the line into sections for youth, maturity, and old age and estimating the year of life according to the position of the marking near the start, middle, or finish of the 20-to-25-year sections.

Judging the Heart Line

• If the heart line starts under the index finger, it shows a normal happy love life that is important to the position in life.

• Starting between the middle and index fingers, it shows a tendency to give your heart away without much thought of the responsibilities of love.

• Starting under the middle finger, it shows a selfish, restricted love life, a materialistic view of emotional attachments.

• When the heart line is long, running nearly all the way across the palm from a start near the side of the palm below the index finger, it shows an idealist in love, one who marries someone above his own status and puts that person on a pedestal.

• Straight and parallel to the head line, it shows a strong emotional control; here romantic attachments often begin with an intellectual friendship.

• Curved and long, it shows warmth and stability in affection, a pleasingly romantic nature.

• Curving upward from the head line, it shows a tendency to give all for love without counting the cost.

• Short, a lack of emotional interests.

• Strong and deep, though short, stability in the affections.

- Chained, broken, wavery—fickleness, many love interests but none stable.
- Faint heart line, faint heart in romantic matters.
- The closer the heart line runs to the base of the index finger, the happier and more stable the marriage. If the line runs all the way to the base of the index finger and links with the ring at the bottom of the finger, the marriage may be impulsive and not good for the position in life.

Special Markings
- A star at the start of the heart line below the index finger gives married happiness.
- A star on the heart line below the index finger or below the ring finger shows a happy marriage at that point in life.
- An island on the heart line shows a period of depression.
- Crosses and breaks show emotional loss—sometimes death of a lover, sometimes the end of an affair.
- Chains on the heart line show emotional tensions.
- Little lines moving upward from the heart line show happiness in love.
- Little lines moving down from the heart line show disappointments in love.
- Doubled, the heart line shows the protection of one who loves you.

The quality of the heart line shows much about your appreciation of the human interests of life, your cultural bent, and love of music and art, which is determined by our feelings. And though the heart line tells about the emotional capacities, other markings must be read to define the sex life, the marriage, and children.

The Quadrangle
The space between the heart line and head line—the quadrangle—shows the breadth of mind and outlook on life. The wider the space, the broader the mind.

These three lines—the lines of life, head, and heart—are the major lines of the palm and divide it into areas that can help you detect the secondary lines, which are sometimes indistinct or missing. These are the line of fate, the line of fame, and the line of health.

THE FATE LINE

The fate line, or line of destiny, begins in the middle of the palm, near the wrist, and runs up the middle of the palm toward the base of the middle finger. The stronger and deeper this line, the more strongly fate controls your life; many breaks and changes of direction in this line indicate that your life often changes through circumstances beyond your control.

Sometimes this line is so strong it dominates the hand at first glance; if other lines are weak and this one strong, it shows a person who is at the mercy of chance. Many persons desire a strong fate line because they prefer to live a life that is beyond their control and responsibility.

Sometimes the fate line is very weak and hard to find, but the three major lines — life, head, and heart — are strong. This person is making his own destiny and his own luck. Such a person may become successful. A truly outstanding person will, however, have strong major lines and a strong line of destiny, too.

Special markings on the fate line — crosses, breaks, squares — show times in life when fate strongly affects you for better or for worse. Use the three time divisions for the period in life when the fateful happening will occur, remembering that the fate line begins in the bottom of the hand and runs toward the fingers, crossing the lines of head and heart on its way.

The fate line is also called the line of destiny, the line of Saturn or Saturn line. This is because it runs to the mount of Saturn below the middle finger (the Saturn finger) and has much to do with the qualities (restrictive) of the planet Saturn. In the occult teachings it is related to *karma* or experience carried over from past lives.

This line tells of the impact of society and world events upon your life, things that come to you from the outside. Doubled, it means that your destiny is guided by another and it doubles your fortune.

44

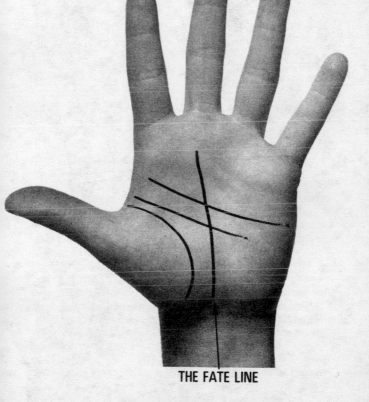

THE FATE LINE

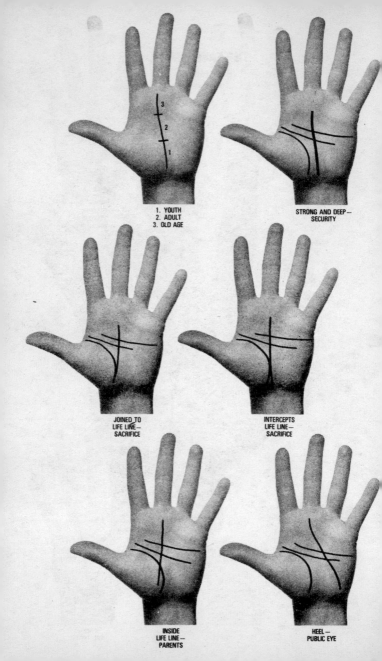

1. YOUTH
2. ADULT
3. OLD AGE

STRONG AND DEEP —
SECURITY

JOINED TO
LIFE LINE —
SACRIFICE

INTERCEPTS
LIFE LINE —
SACRIFICE

INSIDE
LIFE LINE —
PARENTS

HEEL —
PUBLIC EYE

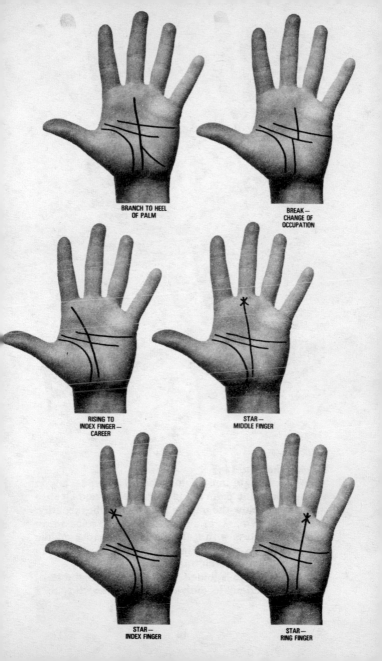

BRANCH TO HEEL
OF PALM

BREAK—
CHANGE OF
OCCUPATION

RISING TO
INDEX FINGER—
CAREER

STAR—
MIDDLE FINGER

STAR—
INDEX FINGER

STAR—
RING FINGER

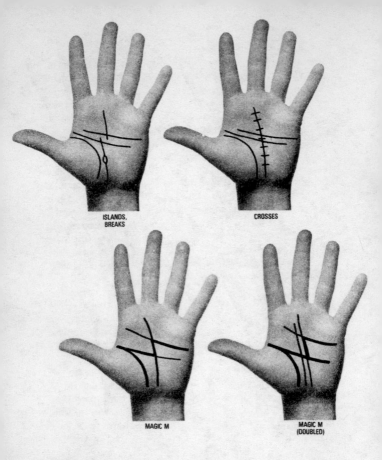

ISLANDS,
BREAKS

CROSSES

MAGIC M

MAGIC M
(DOUBLED)

Judging the Fate Line

- When the fate line begins where it should — low in the middle of the palm — and runs straight and clear to a point just below the middle finger it signifies security. Often it is the mark, in a man, of one who joins a firm early in life, stays with it through a prosperous middle age, and retires well off. In a woman, it often means a secure and comfortable marriage.

- If the fate line is joined to the life line at the start, it shows a self-made individual — one who rises to a position of importance in life by his (or her) own efforts. Such a person often decides very early in life what he or she "will be."

• When it starts free and clear at the wrist and then joins the life line, it means that the person is called upon to surrender his own interests for a time to those of other people. If it later separates from the life line, it means that his life at this point again becomes his own. This configuration is common among young people who have to make detours in their life to help parents or other family members at a time when others of their age are going to college or starting their own family.

• When the fate line starts on the base of the thumb, within the curve of the life line, it shows the opposite situation. Here, members of the family — or someone otherwise bound emotionally to the person — are helpful and supportive in the career.

• When the fate line begins on the heel of the palm, opposite the base of the thumb, it shows that destiny places you before the public in some way. Again, we have often here the self-made personality — the one who rises from obscurity to his destiny as an entertainer or in politics.

• If a line from the heel of the hand runs to the line of destiny, a romantic interest will influence the destiny — marriage or an affair will put you before the public.

• Will you successfully change jobs in the middle years? You can — if a break occurs in the line of fate at the head line and if the line then goes on at another place.

• If the line of fate rises to the ring finger rather than the middle finger, you are destined for success in the arts.

Special Markings

• A star at the end of the fate line shows that destiny has marked you for success. If the line ends in a star under the ring finger, fate intends you for success in creative fields; if under the index finger, fame elsewhere. Under the middle finger, success after years of hard work.

49

- Islands or breaks in the fate line show periods of hard luck, the times when fate has trouble in store for you.
- Squares on the line of fate show protection from dangers.
- Lines crossing the fate line show times when your destiny is opposed by others.

The Magic M

In some hands, in crossing the lines of head and heart, the line of fate creates with the life line the configuration of a large capital M in the middle of the palm. This is considered to be a sign of marriage in women, of money in a man. In any event, M is a mystic letter, and this symbol in the palm can be considered a fortunate marking. If the fate line is doubled or if the line of fame (the line we deal with next) doubles the cross bar of the M, the good fortune is doubled. A woman will marry twice; a man will be a two-time winner on the lottery.

THE LINE OF FAME

The line of fame — also called line of the sun and the line of success — reinforces the fate line. This line is often missing and when it is, prospects of public renown must be read elsewhere in the hand. Usually, the line of fame starts on the heel of the hand, opposite the thumb, and runs vertically up the palm to below the ring finger, paralleling the line of fate.

This line has to do with the rewards of publicity that accompany success — fame, publication, accomplishment in the arts, political popularity, and so forth. Those who lack this line may find success but have to do without the gratifications of public acclaim. The lack of this line can also indicate a lack of gratification from the life effort. Success may be bitter. Time events on this line by using the area below the head line as youth, the area between the head and heart lines as middle years, and the area above the heart line as age.

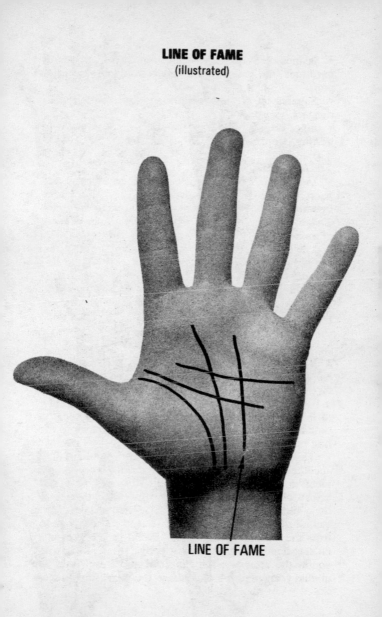

LINE OF FAME
(illustrated)

LINE OF FAME

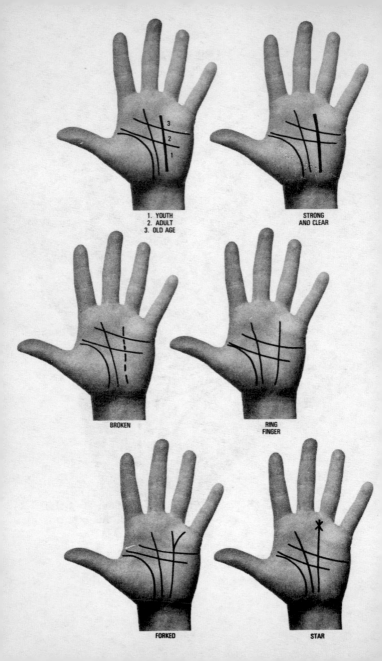

1. YOUTH
2. ADULT
3. OLD AGE

STRONG AND CLEAR

BROKEN

RING FINGER

FORKED

STAR

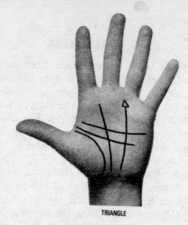

TRIANGLE

Judging the Line of Fame

• The presence of the line on the palm indicates some degree of public life, success, and good fortune. The one with this line cannot live in total obscurity.

• When strong and clearly marked, it indicates both distinction and satisfaction from the life work.

• When broken, it shows the ups and downs of public acknowledgment at the points where the line comes and goes.

• Rising to the ring finger, this line brings fame in the arts.

• Starting from the head line and running through the heart line, it shows hard work for success late in life. Ending in a fork, it makes the success dubious in value.

Special Markings

• If this line ends beneath the ring finger in a star or a triangle, it shows spectacular success in the art fields —writer, musician, painter, showman. A square means a kindly patron.

• Look to see if the line of fame makes a double bar on the magic M of the palm. If it does, good fortune is doubled.

THE HEALTH LINE

Health is wealth. Or so it would seem from palmistry. The line of health has as much to do with achievement of material wealth as it does with physical well-being. Perhaps more, for those in whom the line of health is missing, health is presumed to be good. But it is here, particularly for those who are missing strong lines of fate and fame, that success, particularly in making money, can be evaluated.

The line of health starts below the little finger and runs slantwise across the palm toward the base of the thumb, sometimes joining up with the life line. The point at which the health line joins the life line is often regarded as the end of life-even if the life line continues much longer. Breaks, islands, crosses in this line indicate times when the health needs care. In judging the period when special health hazards come into play, remember that the health line starts below the little finger and runs *down* the palm. The top of the line indicates youth; the middle, adulthood; the bottom, age.

Judging the Health Line

- If this line is missing, there are no health problems.
- Strong and straight, this line shows good business sense as well as the vitality to work hard at making money.
- Wavery—health problems, perhaps rising from nervous tension.
- ˙ Broken or chained, the indications are that poor health will cause business problems.
- Cross lines show danger of accidents.
- A branch to tie in with the life line shows a threat to life from illness in old age.
- A square on the health line shows protection— perhaps good medical treatment or help in a business crisis.
- An island indicates hospitalization.

The Lucky Triangle

Because health and wealth are tied with the life force

THE HEALTH LINE
(illustrated)

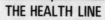

THE HEALTH LINE

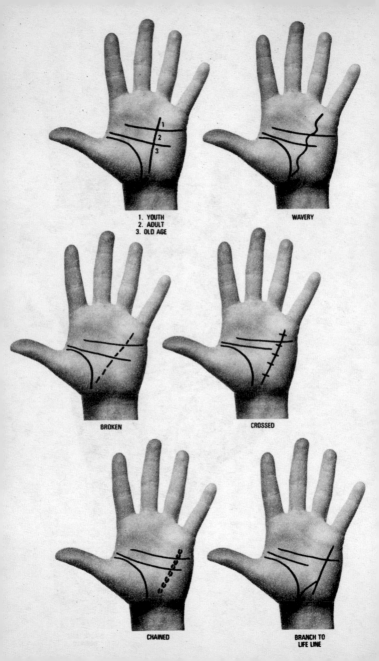

1. YOUTH
2. ADULT
3. OLD AGE

WAVERY

BROKEN

CROSSED

CHAINED

BRANCH TO
LIFE LINE

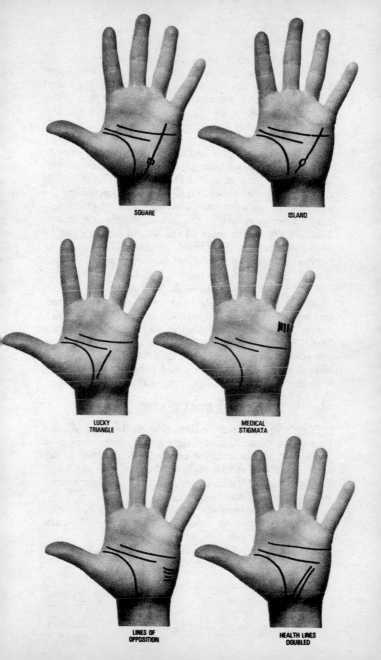

SQUARE

ISLAND

LUCKY
TRIANGLE

MEDICAL
STIGMATA

LINES OF
OPPOSITION

HEALTH LINES
DOUBLED

and the intelligence to produce a fortunate life, the triangle sometimes formed by these lines — life, head, health — is considered an important configuration and is called the lucky triangle. The broader the area of the triangle, the better the luck. The triangle is luckiest of all if the health line touches neither the line of life nor the line of head.

The health line is also called the liver line, the hepatic line, and the line of business. Sometimes it is doubled, and its sister line is called the cephalic line, the Via Lascivia, or the Milky Way. Doubling increases the prospect of success but also promises prodigality — easy come, easy go in the moneymaking syndrome. Much of the significance of the line of health must be read from the rest of the hand — whether it is a physical, nervous, square, spade-shaped, conic, or pointed hand. The very presence of a line of health in a hand is significant — and it should be carefully studied.

Just as the three major lines — the lines of life, head, and heart — show your approach to the world (vitality, mental set, emotional capacity), so the three secondary lines — fate, fame, health — show the world's effect on you (success, public acclaim, material gain). The minor lines show special attributes and events in the life and, with the special markings, reveal the life experience.

THE BRACELETS

The bracelets are the lines that circle the wrist and base of the palm. Usually these are considered signs of good luck. If a bracelet at the base of the palm points at the middle of the hand, it is, however, a health warning. Some say it indicates an inheritance if it connects with the destiny, or fate line.

Bracelets are judged this way: One brings luck; two, better luck; three or more, the best. A half bracelet shows luck that gives out at middle life.

Length of life is sometimes judged from the bracelets: Give yourself 25 years for each bracelet.

THE BRACELETS
(illustrated)

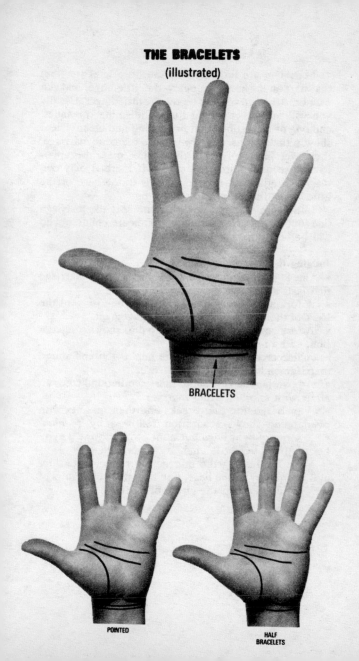

BRACELETS

POINTED

HALF BRACELETS

MARRIAGE AND CHILDREN

Marriages are indicated by the little lines (or line) that start on the hand just below the little finger and run over onto the pad of flesh below the little finger. Usually you will find several light lines, indicating romances, and one or more lines that are strong and clear. These show actual unions. If there is more than one marriage, the lower line represents the earlier one; the upper lines, a second, third, and so on. If there is only one marriage indicated, the nearer it is to the base of the little finger, the later in life it will be.

Little lines that run down to intersect the marriage line (but do not cross through it) indicate children who will be born to the marriage.

Judging the Marriage Lines

• One long clear marriage line shows a happy marriage that lasts a lifetime.

• A fork at the start of the marriage line (toward the back of the hand) shows a long engagement.

• A fork at the end (toward the palm) shows a separation, with or without divorce.

• A line crossing the marriage line at the end shows marriage ending in death or divorce.

• An overlapped or double marriage line indicates an affair with another while married.

• A marriage line that breaks and then resumes with overlapping shows separation followed by reunion.

• A series of light lines but none strong shows a number of affairs but little chance of marriage.

When evaluating the marriage prospects, consider also the quality of the heart line and other indicators of luck in love, such as the girdle of Venus.

MARRIAGE AND CHILDREN
(illustrated)

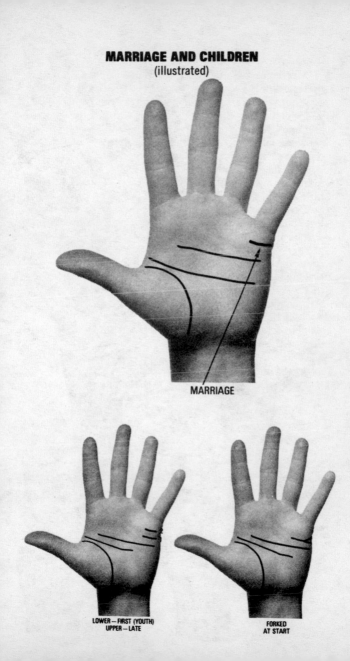

MARRIAGE

LOWER—FIRST (YOUTH)
UPPER—LATE

FORKED
AT START

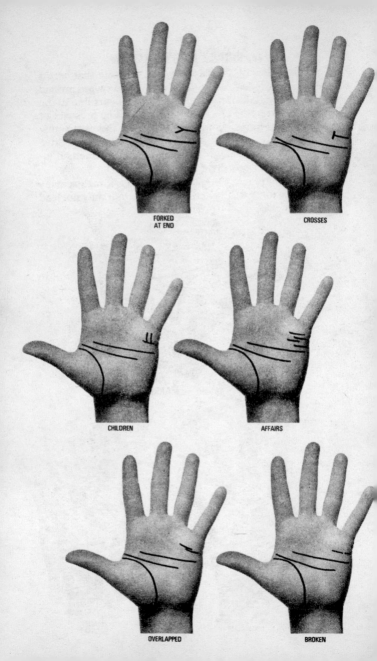

FORKED
AT END

CROSSES

CHILDREN

AFFAIRS

OVERLAPPED

BROKEN

THE GIRDLE OF VENUS

The girdle of Venus is a semicircular line that begins between the index and middle fingers and swings around the upper middle of the palm above the heart line to the space between the ring and little finger. The presence of this girdle shows a strong interest in sex and captivating sex appeal. If the girdle is distinct and clear, the sex drive is healthy but the life force may be pretty much all involved with sexual prowess.

If there are many breaks in the girdle, it means many sexual partners and an active sexuality that may not lead to happiness.

THE GIRDLE OF VENUS
(illustrated)

BROKEN

GIRDLE
OF VENUS

TRAVEL LINES

Travel lines start on the edge of the palm at the heel of the hand, opposite the thumb. One well-marked travel line shows that you will travel far to make your home in a new location. Usually, travel lines show major journeys — overseas, cross-country, or those that have a profound effect on the life of the person. Many light lines can indicate a jet-setter — someone who hops about but with no particular effect on the life. Length and strength of the lines show the distance travelled and the importance of the trip.

• When a travel line intersects the life line, a trip will be made for reasons of health or the health will be affected by a journey.

• Lines criss-crossing the travel lines show danger in travel or problems in travel.

• Squares on these lines show protection from danger.

• Overlaps or breaks show delays.

• When a travel line crosses the line of fate, it means that your life will be changed by the trip.

TRAVEL LINES
(illustrated)

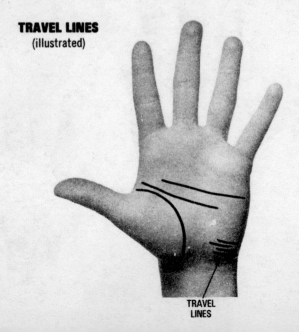

TRAVEL
LINES

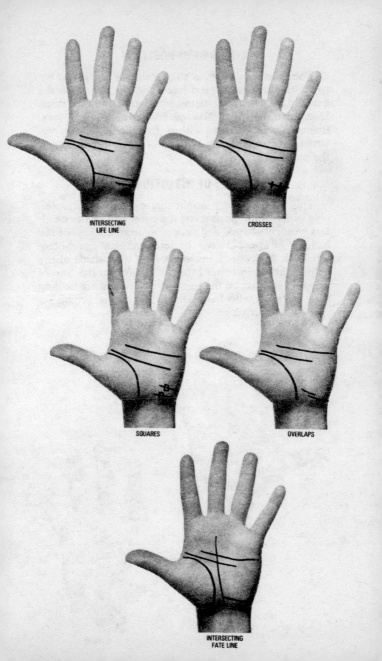

INTERSECTING
LIFE LINE

CROSSES

SQUARES

OVERLAPS

INTERSECTING
FATE LINE

LINES OF OPPOSITION

These lines appear on the outside of the palm, between the heart and head lines, and run over into the quadrangle, the area between heart and head lines. Lines of opposition show putdowns, opposing forces, that one must contend with in the encounters of life. Often they accompany a battle cross in the middle of the palm.

LINE OF INTUITION

This line, showing insight that exceeds the reasonable expectation, appears on the outer part of the palm. It is crescent-shaped and swoops up from the heel of the hand to the area between the heart and head line. Sometimes it is backwards, bulging toward the outside of the palm rather than toward the middle. When the line of intuition appears on the palm, you know you are dealing with someone who has ESP or the next best thing—a sensitive, intuitive person.

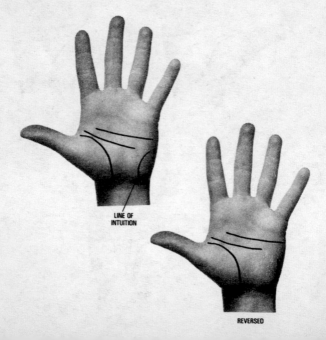

LINE OF
INTUITION

REVERSED

LINE OF ESCAPE

This is in reality a "line of influence," the general heading for lines that originate on the base of the thumb, within the life line, and radiate out to affect events in the life. The line of escape shows an individual who escapes from the problems of life into the imagination and sometimes into the creative arts, if it connects with the line of fortune (fame); into drugs or drinking, if it connects with the line of health or the cephalic line, and sometimes presages suicide, when connected with the line of health.

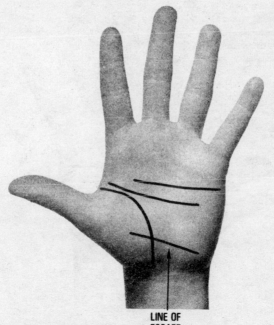

LINE OF
ESCAPE

LINES OF INFLUENCE

These lines, of which the line of escape is one, radiate from the base of the thumb into various parts of the palm. They tick off events at the point at which they touch another line — the line of health, of fate, of fame, and so forth. Most important about the influence lines is whether they originate in family lines or elsewhere in the palm. Most highly regarded of the influence lines are those that show how and where you will get money.

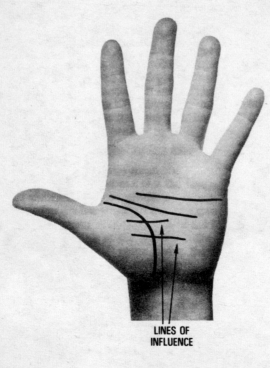

LINES OF INFLUENCE

MONEY LINES

Success, material wealth, security can be found in the lines of fame, health, and fate, but there are other special lines (influence lines) that are found in some hands that can indicate skill at acquiring cash and how it can be done.

• A natural moneymaker is shown by a line that runs from the base of the thumb to below the index finger and ends in a star. This person has the golden touch.

• Wealth that comes from inheritance or family allowances is shown by a line from the base of the thumb to below the little finger.

• Money made in business is shown in a line from the base of the thumb to below the middle finger.

• Money that comes as a surprise and through luck is shown by a line that runs from the head line to below the ring finger, cutting across the line of fame.

MONEY LINES
(illustrated)

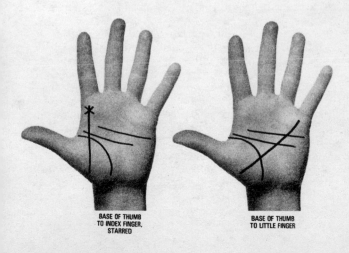

BASE OF THUMB
TO INDEX FINGER,
STARRED

BASE OF THUMB
TO LITTLE FINGER

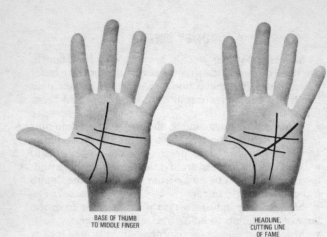

BASE OF THUMB
TO MIDDLE FINGER

HEADLINE,
CUTTING LINE
OF FAME

SPECIAL MARKINGS

Some hands are relatively clear and smooth, with only the major lines clearly marked; other hands are a patchwork of tiny lines and special markings that in themselves have significance. Clear, smooth hands indicate a clear, smooth life with few problems. Lines fretting the palm show many events and much nervous tension.

Sometimes special markings are directly connected with the lines, as we have seen. Such markings show events connected with the area of life that the line governs. Other special markings are sort of free-floaters on the palm and have certain specific connotations depending upon where they appear. Thus, chains, islands, crosses, squares, stars that appear on a line are directly related for good or ill to the context of the line. Chains, in general, denote disturbances; islands or circles, confinement; triangles, good fortune; squares, protection; crosses, opposition; stars, unusual events (lucky, except on the life line); breaks, a change of direction. Tassels or forks at the end of a line show deterioration or dispersion.

The free-floating marks are found in various places

on the palm — on the fleshy pads below the fingers, the heel of the palm, the base of the thumb, or in the triangle or the quadrangle. Here you might find the fortunate squares, triangles, and stars; the unhappy crosses and also grids (crossworks of tiny lines) or a series of little lines, vertical or horizontal. The grids indicate opposition in the area in which they appear; the series of lines show unusual grit and determination in that area of life.

There are two special crosses that should be looked for in the palm, for they have much bearing on the fate of the individual when they appear:

• The battle cross may appear within the triangle formed by the lines of life, head, and health. In times past this was considered the mark of one who would die in battle — a hero's death. Today it indicates someone who may sacrifice himself for a cause in war or peace but also one who lives recklessly or fights life and creates quarrels and opposition.

• The mystic cross is found in the quadrangle — in the middle of the palm between the lines of head and heart. When present it shows someone who will be extremely interested, and probably involved, in the occult and who may sacrifice material goals for spiritual attainment.

The Ring of Solomon

When the mystic cross is present, look also for the ring of Solomon. This is a line that circles the base of the index finger, running from the space between the index and middle fingers to the outside of the palm, sometimes tying in with the heart line. This is a sign of great spiritual potential even if only unconsciously developed. According to ancient lore, King Solomon had a ring that gave him the power to speak with animals; this is it.

The Ring of Saturn

This ring appears at the space between the index finger and the middle (Saturn) finger and loops below it to the space between middle and ring fingers. Do not confuse it with the more widely spaced girdle of Venus.

The ring of Saturn gives restriction and often depression. It is infrequently seen.

The Thumb Chain

Another special marking is a chained line that runs down the middle of the thumb from the area where it joins the palm toward the bottom of the thumb. It is a sign of stubbornness—a quality that can cause much unhappiness to its possessor.

SPECIAL MARKINGS
(illustrated)

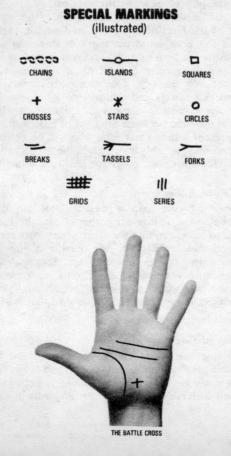

CHAINS   ISLANDS   SQUARES

CROSSES   STARS   CIRCLES

BREAKS   TASSELS   FORKS

GRIDS   SERIES

THE BATTLE CROSS

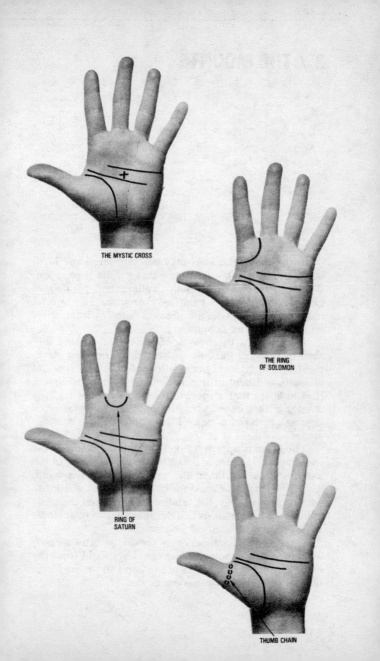

THE MYSTIC CROSS

THE RING
OF SOLOMON

RING OF
SATURN

THUMB CHAIN

3 / THE MOUNTS

In the palm, the lines may be considered the highways (and byways) — the course that the life is set upon. But there are also the mounts, valleys, and plains that give the map of the palm its character. The special markings on the palm are then its "sites of interest" — its motels and its detours.

The mounts, by their development or lack of it — their firmness or flabbiness, their "drift" or even placement — show traits of personality and character, special interests and bent of the individual. If well-developed, they indicate that a specific trait or group of traits is strong; if thin or missing, the trait is in abeyance; a depression shows a lack of development in a specific area.

The mounts appear as pads on the palm under the four fingers, at the base of the thumb, on the heel of the hand, and at the inner and outer sides of the hand. These mounts are named for the planets and, for those who know astrology, the relationship between the traits indicated by the mounts and the character of the planets as traditionally given will be clear.

Lines and special markings should be read in connection with the mounts; lines running to and from the mounts to the various lines of the hand show the direction of interest and experience.

THE MOUNTS
(illustrated)

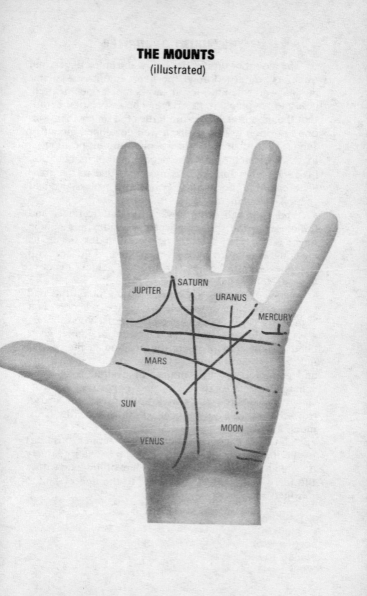

JUPITER SATURN URANUS MERCURY MARS SUN VENUS MOON

THE MOUNT OF JUPITER

The mount of Jupiter lies below the index finger, and often, as you now know, the heart line arises on this mount. And when it does, it shows much open-heartedness and happiness in marriage. The association here is that the mount of Jupiter underlies the finger that rules one's position in life. Thus, a well-developed mount of Jupiter firmly fleshed shows pleasure in position, a joyous approach to life, the acceptance of its bounties. Like the planet Jupiter, this mount is tied to the great benefits of life, hospitality, honor, the professions, and general abundance.

• When this pad drifts toward the middle finger and lies closer to the space between the index and middle finger rather than directly below the index finger, its meaning is a more conservative kind of living, with steadiness and directness toward the achievements of a more solid kind of living.

• When soft and overly broad and cushiony, this pad can show tremendous self-indulgence, success that comes too easily, or wasting of material goods.

• A triangle on a firm "good" mount of Jupiter gives good fortune and protects the position in life; a star indicates great happiness in home and married life and good fortune in winning an exalted position; a square protects against loss and opposition; a cross shows that desired goals may not be realized; a grid, excessive drive and egotism; a series of little lines, much ambition.

• A line that runs from the mount of Jupiter (position) to the line of the head can show a personality largely devoted to making money; to the line of life, one whose life force is guided by ambition; to the line of fate, a destined success.

THE MOUNT OF JUPITER
(illustrated)

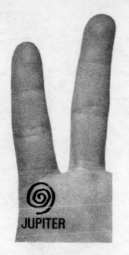

JUPITER

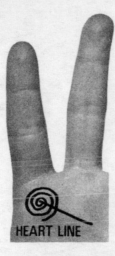

HEART LINE

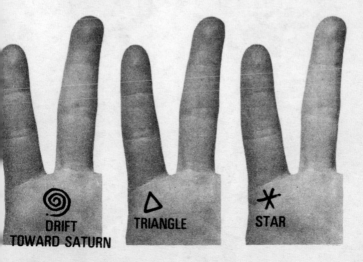

DRIFT
TOWARD SATURN

TRIANGLE

STAR

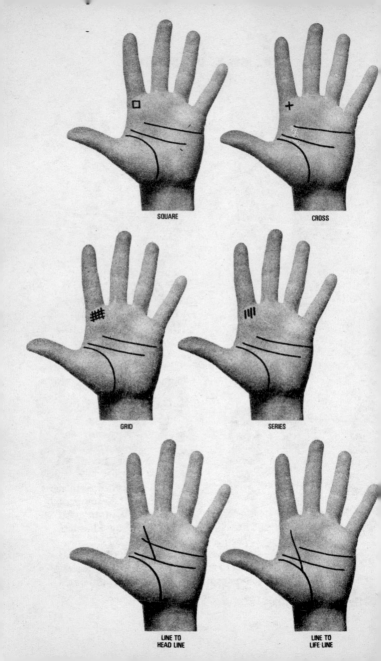

SQUARE

CROSS

GRID

SERIES

LINE TO
HEAD LINE

LINE TO
LIFE LINE

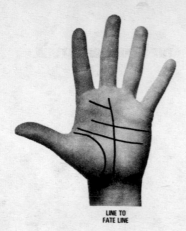

**LINE TO
FATE LINE**

THE MOUNT OF SATURN

Here is a spot where absence of the mount is the preferred characteristic. The mount of Saturn, if it is developed, lies directly below the middle finger. This is the finger that represents restrictions, duty, and to some extent hard work and business. The line of fate, as you know, is directed toward this finger. Fate shows us our *karma*, or responsibilities in our lifetime. That is why this area so often shows restrictions.

Rather than a well-developed mount directly below the finger, most persons have a flat area — a plain or a valley — between the adjoining mounts of Jupiter and Uranus. This shows a fortunate absence of the characteristics indicated by a well-developed mount of Saturn.

• When firm and well-developed, the mount of Saturn indicates the misogynist — a hater of people, a lover of solitude and bitter thoughts; though there is often good in the person somewhere, he will hate to show kindness or affection and is hard indeed to love.

• When large, soft and cushiony a developed mount of Saturn shows one given to morbid thoughts and fantasies.

• If the heart line begins under this finger, it indicates selfishness in love.

THE MOUNT OF SATURN
(illustrated)

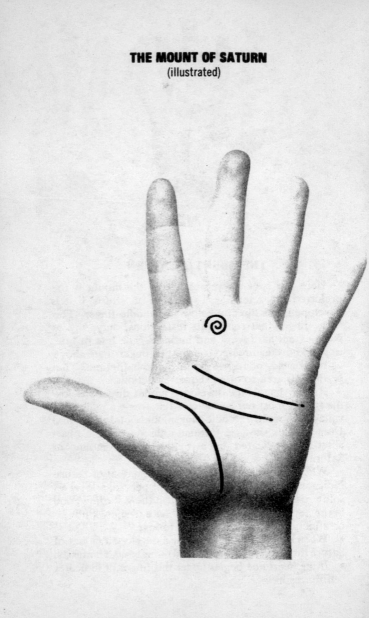

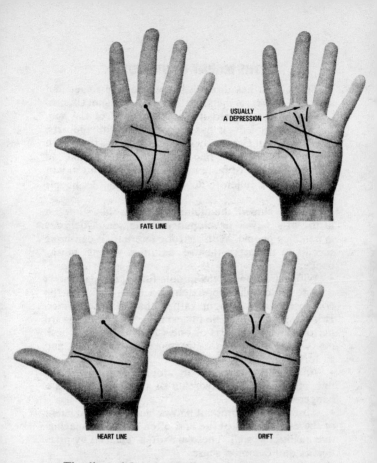

FATE LINE

USUALLY A DEPRESSION

HEART LINE

DRIFT

• The line of fate normally runs to this mount; this shows a person who accepts his fate.

• A star on Saturn indicates a dramatic fate; a cross, danger of accidental death; a square, protection from unkind fate; a grid, depression; a triangle, hidden talent or an interest in the occult. A circle here shows danger of prison or self-isolation.

• When the adjoining mounts drift toward the mount of Saturn the position is stabilized and the creative mind made more realistic.

THE MOUNT OF URANUS

This mount lies directly below the ring finger and modern palmistry assigns it to the new-age planet Uranus. Old palmistry assigned it to Apollo, god of the sun. Take your choice—it has much to do with the arts, ruled in ancient Greece by Apollo. It also has to do with sociability and finer things of life, attributable to Uranus. The line of fame normally ends on this mount —and so it has much to do with the public life, people and prestige.

• Well-developed, the mount of Uranus shows interest in the arts, a well-developed esthetic sense, delicacy in handling people. With a strong fate line, it can bring success in the arts—theatre, painting, writing, music, dance.

• With a drift toward the middle finger, this pad shows a more philosophic approach and often indicates the composer or playwright rather than the performer. Drifting toward the little finger, it inclines more toward performance in the arts or one who goes into the business side of the arts—theatre manager, bookseller, and so forth.

• An overdeveloped or soft mount of Uranus shows one who inclines to daydream of success or who is a hanger-on in the arts.

• Absence of this mount shows lack of development of the esthetic side of life and often a lack of imaginative qualities as well. These are often replaced by practicality and common sense.

• A star on Uranus at the tip of the line of fame indicates that you will shine brightly—perhaps as a star in one of the artistic fields; it can also bring wealth through the arts or can throw you into the company of those who are rich and famous and creative.

• A cross here shows the one who tries hard for success but cannot quite make it; a square is helpful; a grid shows one who pushes for fame (using 125% of his talents); a series of little lines, artistic work for material gain; a triangle, serious endeavors in artistic work that are rewarded.

THE MOUNT OF URANUS
(illustrated)

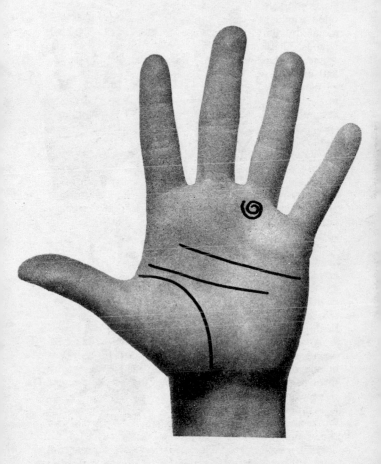

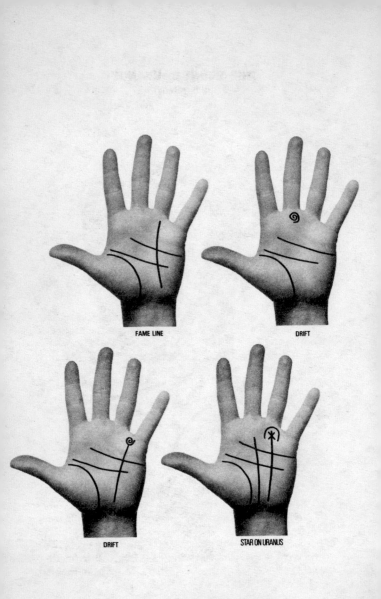

FAME LINE

DRIFT

DRIFT

STAR ON URANUS

• When either the line of fate or the line of fame heads for the ring finger, it indicates success in a career in the arts; starred, it gives spectacular success. Seeing such a configuration, you can discover a hidden talent and perhaps help it to success.

THE MOUNT OF MERCURY

This mount lies below the little finger — and bears the lines of marriage and of children. It has to do with the practical mind, the everyday routine, but also with expression — talking, selling, writing commercially — and science, the healing arts, and commerce. The line of health and success in business starts on the mount of Mercury.

• Well-developed and firm, the mount of Mercury shows a practical and active mind with much business sense and interest in surroundings. Undeveloped, it shows a lack of these characteristics — impracticality, scattered thoughts, and even insincerity. Drifting toward the ring finger, it shows a practical interest in the arts — as buyer, seller, dealer. As we have seen, if the head line points toward this finger, one becomes a collector of things or information.

• A series of vertical lines on this mount show ability in the healing arts — one who can take care of the health of others as doctor, nurse, social worker.

• A grid here shows instability in mind or physical health; a triangle gives success in business; a circle indicates that one will go around in circles; a cross here is the sign of the double-dealer; a star gives distinction in science, medicine, business; a square helps in making split-second decisions.

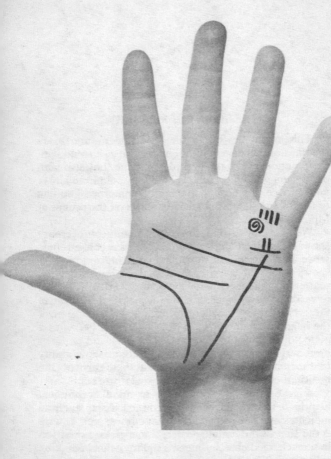

THE MOUNT OF THE MOON

The mount of the moon lies at the heel of the hand opposite the thumb. This is the area of imagination and creativity. The line of fame begins on this mount and rises to the ring finger — imagination thus leads to fame in the arts and all creative endeavors. Here too, on the moon's mount, we find the lines of travel, indications of the journeys of the mind and of the person to faraway places that expand the consciousness with new scenery, new faces, new languages, and new ways. When the line of the head dips toward the mount of the moon, creativity and imagination spark the reason — and this makes for adventurous and creative thinking. But should the line of the head go too deep into the moon's sphere or be starred there, reason may be lost in imagination and great mental instability may result.

• Unconnected to the head line, a star on the moon's mount shows brilliant imagination and the possibility of great mental discoveries through creative thought.

• A cross on this mount makes one suffer through day-dreaming; a square gives protection in travel; a triangle balances the imaginative powers; a grid produces worries and imagined fears.

• Well-developed, this mount shows great imaginative faculties; thin, weak, pale — imaginative faculties are poor indeed.

THE MOUNT OF THE MOON
(illustrated)

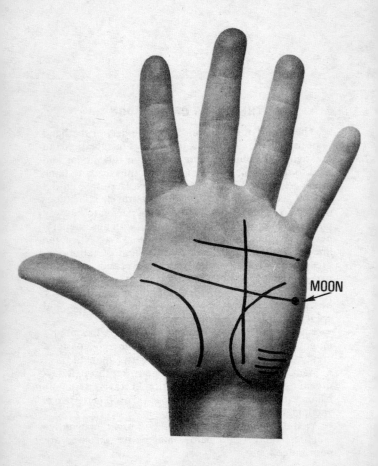

MOON

THE MOUNT OF VENUS

The mount of Venus lies at the base of the thumb and is circled by the life line, to which it is closely related. Venus shows the physical love nature, the strength and quality of the physical desires and is also related to the higher mind, particularly in women. Unless other qualities in the hand incline her toward fickleness in love, the well-developed mount of Venus, firm and broad, shows a kind and womanly nature as well as physical vitality and sexuality.

The spread of this mount of Venus has much to do with the swoop of the life line. If the line swings down the mid-palm, the area of Venus is roomy and gives the love nature scope; if the life line cramps this area, one will be cautious in love and life; vitality too will suffer.

• When the mount of Venus is overfleshed and firm, it shows a person controlled by the sex drive; if too soft and full, someone who may be victim of his (oftener her) sexuality.

• Stars, triangles, or squares on this mount show successes in love; grids or crosses show frustrations.

• Often lines (influence) run from this part of the palm to the various fingers; these show how the love nature is used in life. A line running to the index finger shows sex being used for position and power; to the middle finger, restrictions through physical love; to the ring finger, sexual motivation in the arts; to the little finger, many sexual partners.

THE MOUNT OF VENUS
(illustrated)

VENUS

THE MOUNT OF THE SUN

The mount of the sun lies directly below the middle joint of the thumb. A fatty protuberance here shows a fat ego — perhaps an excess of success to gratify conceit. Firm and full, it shows success through good determination and will. Flattened, it shows a diminished self-image and lack of success through insecurity.

• Squares, triangles, stars on this mount are further indications of fame and success and much self-advantage.
• A grid shows anxieties that interfere with success; a cross, frustrations of the ego drive.

THE MOUNTS OF MARS

Mars has twin mounts — one on each side of the palm. Both have to do with courage, will, and the aggressive drive. One lies on the inside of the palm, above the thumb and just below the life line. This mount shows the active aggression, the amount of fight. The other mount lies on the outside of the palm, opposite the thumb and above the mount of the moon, between the head and heart lines. This mount rules self-control, the ability to govern the aggressive instincts and use them wisely.

• The inner mount of Mars is related to the life line and has much to do with the life force. Overdeveloped, it makes for too much aggressiveness and a tendency to pick quarrels; underdeveloped, a lack of the power of self-defense.
• The outer mount of Mars is best when the lines of head and heart run parallel to enclose it. Here the self-control mediates between the feelings and the mind and gives balance and maturity. Well-developed and firm, the mount shows strong self-control without rigidity; too soft and full, self-control is weakened; too firm, the control can be exhausting.
• A star on either of these mounts shows achievements by one's own will; a square, protection from attackers; a circle or island, danger from sneak attacks; crosses or a grid, secret and open enemies.

- For competitive sports, well-developed mounts of Mars are a great asset.

THE MOUNT OF THE SUN & THE MOUNTS OF MARS
(illustrated)

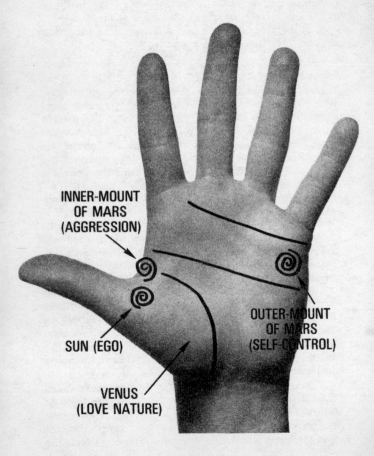

INNER-MOUNT
OF MARS
(AGGRESSION)

SUN (EGO)

VENUS
(LOVE NATURE)

OUTER-MOUNT
OF MARS
(SELF-CONTROL)

4 / THE PALM AND THE THUMB

THE HOLLOW PALM

A hollow palm is sometimes considered an asset because "nothing will drop out of it." More realistically, it is a symbol of caution and fear, carefulness that is excessive, the sign of one who "plays it safe." The trouble with playing it safe is that one rarely will play for keeps and often won't play at all. The flatter the inside of the palm, the more generous and outgoing the nature, the more accepting the person, the less likely the person is to be suspicious or to hold grudges.

This flattish mid-area of the palm is called the plain of Mars (it lies between the two mounts of Mars). It is here that we find the battle cross, lying within the triangle (luck) formed by the lines of head, life, and health. The lower plain of Mars has to do with the individual's struggle to control his animal nature and aggressiveness.

The quadrangle (the area between the head and heart lines) is the upper section of the plain of Mars. Here the ego struggles to control the emotions and we find in this area the mystic cross, which shows a spiritual victory. Like the area of the triangle — the broader the better — the wider and more fully spaced the quadrangle is, the more fortunate for the individual.

Though revealing in themselves, the lines and mounts take on full meaning only when related to the hand as a whole — its shape, flexibility, color, its proportions, the shape and relative length of the fingers, the size and thickness and flexibility of the thumb. In fact, the depth and clarity of the lines — what is normal for a particular hand — must be judged in relation to the hand type. Variations from the normal are also important, but they become more or less significant in a hand when related to its basic type. Equally important to the character and the natural bent of the personality is the thumb.

THE THUMB

Nothing is more important to our handiness — and our everyday character — than the thumb. Consider that such an experience as grasping a pinch of salt would be impossible without our well-developed thumb. The operation of scissors depends completely upon it. Anything that must be grasped — such as a hammer — takes thumb-work. The development of the human thumb has been closely tied to the development of the brain and eye. In palmistry the development of the thumb is related to the will.

The ideal thumb for character and sensitivity — humanness — is one that is reasonably long (it should reach close to the middle joint of the index finger when laid against the side of the palm), shapely — firm and well-proportioned in the upper section and slightly "waisted," or slimmed, at the mid section, and moderately flexible. When the hand is spread, the thumb should stand apart from the palm a reasonable distance but not too far (if the index finger were considered to point north, the well-balanced thumb points northwest) and should not be rigid (it should be possible to spread the thumb some distance away from the fingers with easy pressure and to bend the top joint backward somewhat, but in neither case so far that the thumb makes a right angle with its base). Such a thumb indicates a person who is well-balanced in his will, logic, and love nature.

• The wider the angle that is made when the thumb is pushed away from the palm and the index finger, the more generous the person. This is known as the "angle of generosity." A stiff thumb that sticks to the side of

THE THUMB
(illustrated)

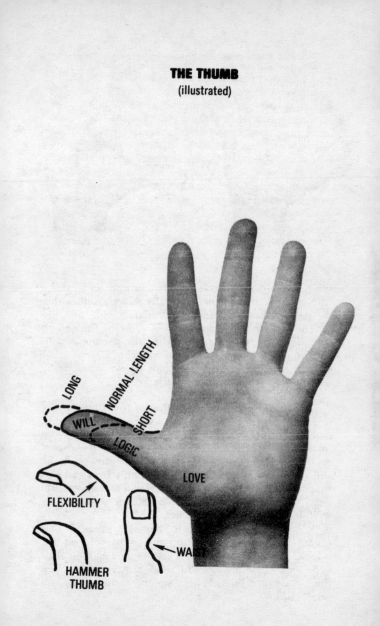

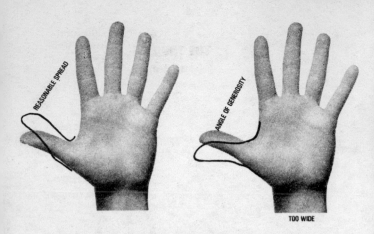

REASONABLE SPREAD — ANGLE OF GENEROSITY

TOO WIDE

the palm shows someone who is cautious and careful with cash. A thumb that naturally hides itself within the palm shows fearfulness and anxiety.

• The farther backward the top joint of the thumb can be pushed, the more easygoing the person. A stiff, unyielding thumb shows a rigid nature.

• The reasonably mobile thumb shows adaptability without its owner's being a pushover.

The three segments of the thumb traditionally represent the will (top section); the logic (middle section); and the love nature (bottom section). This bottom joint lies under the mount of Venus, as we have seen.

• If the top section is thin and flat, it shows a weak will and little responsibility; a reasonably firm and well shaped upper section shows normal will and aggressiveness; very full and firm, the top section shows strong willfulness and self-centeredness.

Sometimes you will see a "hammer thumb." This thumb has a top section so firm and overdeveloped that it looks like a hammerhead. This denotes an elemental ego—overwhelmingly willful and materialistic. Such thumbs are rare, but they are a potent warning in human relationships.

• The second section, between the top and middle joints, indicates logic. When very full and heavy, it shows a temperament that forces itself upon others. When very thin, it shows the overdelicate and picky mind; when slightly slimmed in the mid-section, it shows a balanced and logical mind.

• The bottom section, the mount of Venus, shows the animal passions. Compare it with the rest of the thumb. If overdeveloped in comparison with the other joints (it is, of course, normally the longest and fullest, but proportions must be considered), it shows the love nature dominating the will and logic; if flat and thin proportionately, it shows lack of vital force to balance determination and mental set.

Proportions are also important in the thumb; if the upper joints are small in relation to the bottom section, the person is weak-willed; if the top section is extremely long in comparison to the middle section, the will dominates the intellect. If the middle section is unduly long and the top section small and weak, the person will have big ideas and will lack the grit to carry them out. Normal length for a thumb is one that reaches at least halfway up the first joint of the index finger when laid against the side of the hand. A much longer thumb —one that reaches up to the middle joint of the index finger—shows great power of mind and will. A short thumb—one that barely makes it to the first joint of the index finger—shows poor mental development.

The shape of the thumb, and whether the joints are smooth or knotty, also affect the will-logic-love nature. Pointed and smooth jointed, the thumb indicates an impulsive nature; square and smooth, realism; wide at the tip (but not clubbed) and with heavy joints, imagination; square and knotty, much practicality but experimental.

5 / THE FINGERS

The fingers (and the thumb) must, of course, be judged in relation to the entire hand. But they also should be evaluated singly and in relation to each other. And because we so often encounter a "mixed hand" — one with fingers of various types — and because so many beginners find it hard to identify hand shapes anyway, it is wise to start by trying to understand the fingers.

Fingers are evaluated for their length or shortness in relation to the length of the palm and also in the relation of one finger to another; for their smoothness or their knotty joints; and for their basic shape — pointed, spade-shaped, conical, or square. You will also want to look at the size and shape of the fingernails and to consider the various segments of the finger. Let's start with long or short.

• Fingers are considered long when the longest (usually the middle finger) is as long as the palm itself. Normally the longest finger is about seven-eighths the length of the palm. Short fingers are simply shorter than this. Of course, a long hand can have longer fingers than a short square hand, so this relative length to the length of the palm must be your guide.

• Long, slim fingers show the mind controlling the emotional and aggressive nature; short, heavy fingers show the physical nature ruling the higher mind. But emotionally very good people can have relatively short, thick fingers. What the hand is telling you here is whether the individual is an intellectual, emotional, or physical thinker.

FINGER CHARACTERISTICS
(illustrated)

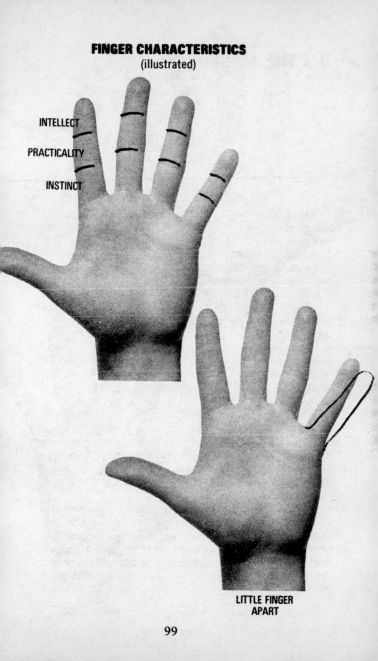

INTELLECT

PRACTICALITY

INSTINCT

LITTLE FINGER
APART

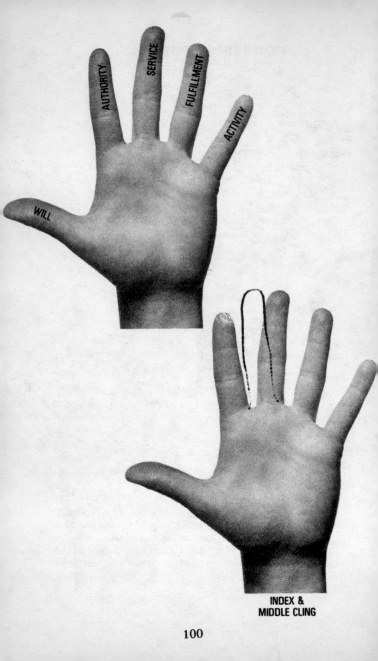

AUTHORITY

SERVICE

FULFILLMENT

ACTIVITY

WILL

**INDEX &
MIDDLE CLING**

100

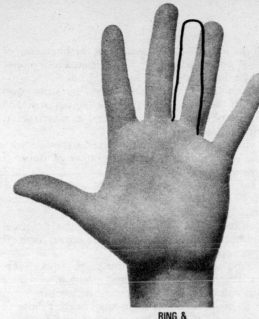

**RING &
MIDDLE CLING**

Length must also be considered in the relation of each finger to the others on the hand. We have seen that the thumb normally reaches to well above the bottom joint of the index finger. The index finger, for its part, normally reaches about a third of the way up the nail of the middle finger — to about the middle of the upper-most joint (view the hand from the back to evaluate this).

• Longer than this, the index finger shows a tendency to dominate others; much shorter, it means that you let others control you.

• The ring finger should reach just above the start of the nail of the middle finger — about halfway on the upper-most joint. When it is much longer than this, it can indicate artistic talent but also a kind of recklessness.

• The little finger should make it to the top joint of the ring finger. Much shorter, it shows a lack of influence of the practical mind; much longer, great ability in talking, writing, selling, and such.

Each finger, as we have seen from the character of the mounts on the palm below it, is related to a planet and to the areas of life ruled by that planet.

• The index finger, the Jupiter finger, rules the good things of life, the ability to acquire position and material wealth, control over others, happiness in marriage. It also represents authority.

• The middle finger, the Saturn finger, has to do with vocation, restrictions, and the operation of duty. It represents service.

• The ring finger, Uranus, has to do with the artistic elements of life, fame, publicity, success. It represents fulfillment.

• The little finger, Mercury, governs the practical mind and health, commercial ventures, and so forth. It represents activity.

When evaluating the fingers for shape, smoothness of joints, length of segments, and position, consider the affairs ruled by the finger in your delineation.

• Look to how the fingers stand apart or cling close to the neighboring finger(s) when the hand is relaxed.

• If the little finger stands apart from the others with much space between it and the ring finger, it shows an independent mind.

• If the ring finger (Uranus) clings to the middle finger (Saturn), it shows that the arts are related to the life work and that fate will take part in any success.

• If the index finger (Jupiter) and the middle finger cling together, it shows that you will gain position and authority through your vocation. If these fingers stand apart from each other, it shows position comes from other means.

The shape of the individual fingers tells much about the area of life in which the person is active or passive. So does the smoothness or knottiness of the joints and which joints are smooth and which knotty.

In each finger, the top section is said to denote intellect; the middle section, practicality; the lower section, instinct. This character must be related to the affairs governed by the individual finger. If, for example, the top section of the little finger is the longest segment, it shows intellect dominating the practical mind; if the middle section of the ring finger is the longest segment of that finger, practicality governs artistic ventures; if the lowest section of the index finger is the longest, it shows instinct governing the rise to power. The longest section of the middle finger will show whether intellect, practicality, or instinct governs the life work.

In the same way, the smoothness or knottiness of the joints relates to the affairs of the finger and the working of the instinct, practicality, or intellect in the fulfillment of what the finger denotes.

• Smooth joints show passivity, even carelessness, and a tendency to be ruled by impulse in activities.
• Knotty joints show struggle. If the top joints of the fingers are smooth and the middle joints knotty, this shows a person whose practicality and intellect work smoothly together but who has to apply himself to utilize his instincts in the service of practicality. Well-developed knuckles show strong but controlled instinctive drive.
• The fleshiness of the pads on the inside of the fingers or the flatness and thinness of the area indicates development or lack of it in the characteristics related to the finger and its segments. Well developed balls on the top segment of the fingers, for example, show highly developed intellect and an innate courtesy of mind; flatness on any of these fingers would mean a lack of intellectual insight in the field the finger represents.

The shape of the fingers should normally be related to the shape of the whole hand. That is, a square hand should have square fingers; a pointed hand, pointed fingers; a cone-shaped hand, long, smooth, tubular fingers; a spade-shaped hand, fingers that are broad and thick at the tips. But many hands have mixed finger types and these require individual analysis. A person with such mixed fingers is often a person of great diversity and varied talents — an interesting individual with many aspects and qualities.

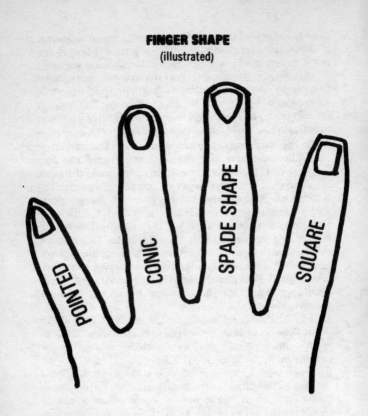

POINTED CONIC SPADE SHAPE SQUARE

• Square, a finger shows realism and down-to-earthness in the area of life controlled by the finger; pointed, the finger shows great artistic sense in the area ruled by the specific finger; spade-shaped (wide at the tip), the finger shows inventiveness; cone-shaped (tubular). the finger shows imagination. Thus a person with a square ring finger (Uranus) would show much practicality in use of artistic talents; but combined with pointed index finger, little prowess in relation to position in life.
• The straightness or crookedness of the fingers needs

to be evaluated, too. Straight fingers show one who is straight-forward, direct, honest, and clear-headed. Crooked, the finger shows deviousness or some mis-shaping in the area of the personality controlled by the twist.

The size and shape of the fingernails are also useful in evaluating the hand and identifying the type of finger. The pointed finger has an almond-shaped nail, round and broad at the base and tapering toward the finger tip; the cone-shaped finger has an oval nail; the square finger has a broad square nail; the spade-shaped finger has nails with a squarish base that broaden slightly toward the tip.
• Consider the nail bed (not the shaping by the mani-cure of the nail tip) in evaluating the shape and size. Usually a nail occupies the upper half of the top joint of the finger and has a rim of flesh showing around it; a long nail indicates a tender spirit; a short nail, uneasy temperament; wide nail, quarrelsomeness; a narrow nail, refinement of spirit.

6 / HANDS

The shape of the hand can tell you much about the personality, temperament, and way of life of the subject. Nature separates hands into seven basic types — though we deal chiefly with only five — and many variations show up in the length, size, and smoothness of the fingers.

The five hand types in palmistry are the square, the pointed, the conical, the spade-shaped and the mixed hand. Also dealt with is the knotty hand — and sometimes we refer to the "nervous" hand. The elemental hand is rarely seen in palm-reading.

THE SQUARE HAND

The square hand normally has squarish fingers, but these may be long or short, smooth or knotted. The palm of this hand is as wide as it is long, and the base is squared off. Often the hand is smooth and firm, with the lower mounts (moon and Venus) well developed and upper mounts (below the fingers) more or less run together in a firm ridge. The lines are usually few and relatively deep and clear and often comparatively short. Except for the life line, they will be straight, as well — the mark of a realist.

• Traditionally, the square hand is the hand of the worker, and represents a balanced and earthy individual. Today, this hand is found among many successful businessmen — those who have risen from working with their hands. With fairly long, square fingers, the hand shows a tendency to successful enterprise more than with short, square fingers.

• Look in this hand for someone who is engaged in a practical, materialistic occupation and who has solid values and much physical energy.

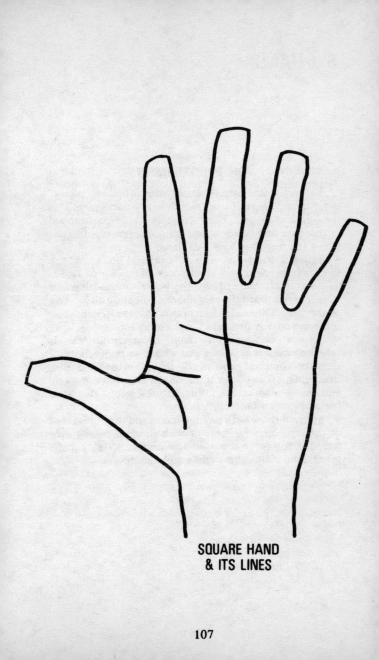

**SQUARE HAND
& ITS LINES**

THE POINTED HAND

This is the hand that is usually described as "pretty" in a woman. Often it has great delicacy and grace. It is the "almond-shaped" hand — slightly wider but rounded at the base and tapering·into smooth, pointed fingers. Often the thumb is long and flexible.

• This is a hand that is usually pale in color and the lines may be clear, but rarely deep. The line of fate is usually clearly marked and the heart or head line, or both, curve toward the ring finger, indicating an interest in the arts. Often the life line is doubled, indicating someone who is protected and cared for.

• This is considered the hand of someone who is relatively useless as a doer and who is an appreciator of the arts; someone who needs to be surrounded with beauty. Often its owner is interested in psychic matters and can be mediumistic. With knotted joints, this hand becomes much more practical.

• Many of those with pointed hands today get involved in the cosmetics business or with the hair-styling arts, which is fortunate, because few people today can be taken care of by others and simply pampered.

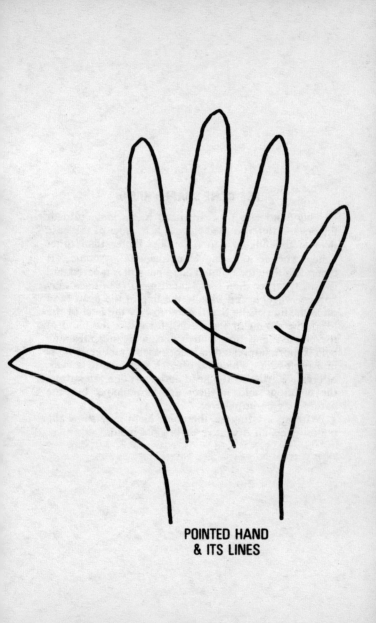

**POINTED HAND
& ITS LINES**

THE CONE-SHAPED HAND

This hand can be recognized by its long, tubular fingers and full, rounded base. It is broader at the base than at the fingers and is far less flatter than other hands, whence its name "cone-shaped" or "conic." It tapers less than the pointed hand but still is tapered and is usually larger than the pointed hand. The lines may be very wavery, and usually the line of the head (and often the line of the heart) point toward the heel of the hand (the mount of the moon), for this is the hand of the creative and imaginative person. It indicates one who is more interested in theory than practice if he is in a profession, which he often is—educator, lawyer, or creative artist. If the head and heart line are strong, the emotions and intellect are harmonious but the nature may be impulsive.

• With knotty fingers, the conic hand may show the philosopher, an inventive or original mind.

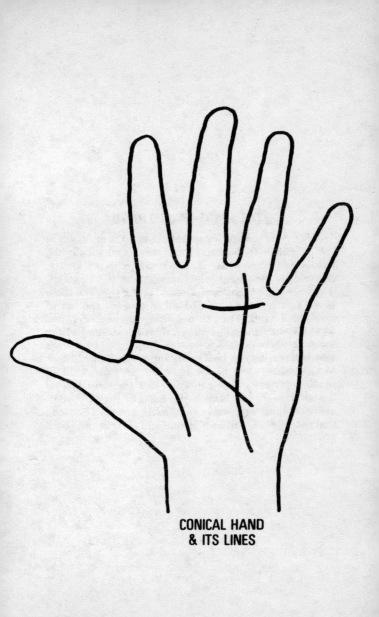

**CONICAL HAND
& ITS LINES**

THE SPADE-SHAPED HAND

The spade-shaped, or spatulate, hand is narrower at the base than at the top of the palm, and usually the base is somewhat squarish. Often the joints are knotty, particularly the finger joints rather than the knuckles. The fingers are broad and squared at the tips, and these fleshy tips act as a special kind of tool for the use of this active hand. They turn screws, remove keys, and so forth, with a kind of magic. This is the hand of the inventor, the mechanical genius. New paths in science and engineering are broken by the spade-shaped hand. Women with such hands have a particular kind of manual dexterity that can confound the most helpful husband. In women, this is the hand of the do-it-yourself decorator and make-it-yourself sewer. The head and heart lines are usually strong and clear in this hand.

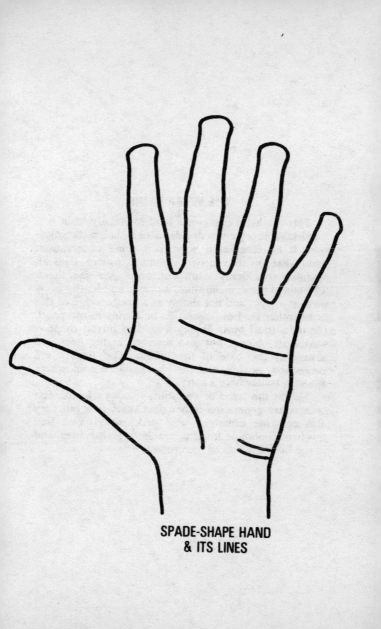

**SPADE-SHAPE HAND
& ITS LINES**

THE MIXED HAND

This is a hand that seems hard to classify — but it is
unmistakable once you decide there is such a classifica-
tion. It is remarkable how, with some observation,
hands that are true to type — pointed, square, conical,
spatulate — suddenly stand out when you see them.
The mixed hand, meanwhile, assumes an identity of its
own, as a type, and not simply as a hodgepodge of this
or the other kind of fingers. To be a truly mixed hand,
the palm itself must display a kind of mixed shape —
somewhat oblong, but also rounded at the heel and
square at the base of the thumb. The fingers are
diversified, as well, and the joints will be somewhere
smooth, somewhere knotty.

• This is the hand of versatility — today's hand. The
owners are generalists rather than specialists but they
also combine creativity with practicality. You find
this hand among journalists, teachers, researchers, and
in the business side of the creative arts.

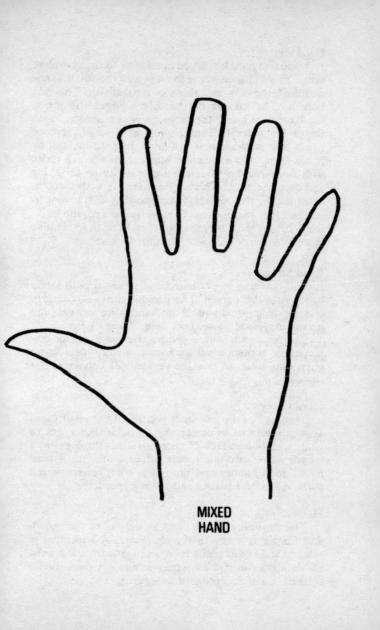

**MIXED
HAND**

115

Hand Size

Hand size must be judged in relation to the complete body. You will soon come to recognize the small hands and the large ones and those of normal size. The rule here is: The smaller the hand, the larger the ideas; the larger the hand, the more eager the person to do things for himself. That people with small, smooth hands are ineffectual is not true. In aptitude testing it has been shown that the best executives are those with no particular talents but the ability to think big and delegate work. This applies to many with smooth, small hands; they delegate because they don't want to do things for themselves. The knotty-handed, the large-handed, may think big, too, but they have an irresistible impulse to carry out their ideas for themselves.

Hand Strength

The best way to evaluate hand strength is to shake hands with the person. The person with a strong grip is trying to impress you; if the handshake is weak, the person may want you to take care of him or her.

Shaking hands with a prospective employer or employee or someone with whom you must deal is an important guide to how the person will behave in the situation.

Hand Color

The color of the palm tells you about the vitality and aggressiveness of its owner. A pale palm shows lack of vitality and often lack of enterprise; a yellow palm, a jaundiced or sardonic nature, often inhibited; a pink palm, good vitality and normal aggressiveness; a red palm, a forceful nature and often hyperactive.

Flexibility

The flexibility of the hand as well as of the thumb and fingers is a key to the character. A hand that is relaxed and bends easily back and forth from the wrist shows a trustful and easygoing nature—a person who is flexible and accepting of new ideas.

- A stiff hand shows a rigid personality.
- If the fingers can be pushed readily all the way back so that they are at right angles to the palm, the person is a pushover. The fingers should be moderately flexible.
- An easily bent thumb shows a similar tendency. A rigid thumb shows strong will.
- The spread of the fingers — the degree to which they can be spread out from each other like a five-pointed star — has much to do with the versatility and breadth of personality. If fingers cling together, the personality will be hampered; if the fingers are cramped and tend to curl inward, the personality, too, is involuted. Spread the thumb away from the fingers and bend it back to see how generous and how flexible is the will.
- As a further delineation, ask the person to make a fist. If the thumb is left sticking out above the fingers, the person will be foolhardy — careless of life and limb. If he or she protects the thumb by curling it inside the fingers, you can recognize the person who will defend himself and more than likely will deliver the first blow when a dispute arises.

Warmth

The warmth of the hand is important, too. If the hand is cool, the individual is likely to be impersonal. Warm hands really do show a warm heart.

We have tried to show the meanings of lines and the mounts and to give "readings" for line variations in lines. The key to complete understanding is knowing the significance of the lines and the meaning of the area toward which a line is directed or the area it joins.

The mounts, fingers, and many of the lines are named for planets, and the character of these planets and the affairs of life they govern are a key to correct interpretation.

7 / ASTROLOGY AND PALMISTRY

If you have a working knowledge of astrology, it helps in understanding the palm. And some knowledge is needed simply because certain areas of the palm and the adjacent fingers are named for planets and carry with them the connotations and qualities these planets are concerned with. For example, you will often be asked certain direct questions as you do your hand-reading. These are answerable only if you know to what parts of the hand the question should be referred.

It is also helpful to know the astrological sun sign of the person whose hand is being read. Today, nearly everyone knows that he or she is a Gemini, Leo, Virgo — or whatever. If the subject also knows his moon position and rising sign, all the better. To find his sun sign (in case he doësn't know it), ask his birthday and place him in the appropriate sun according to birth date.

Because birth signs have certain characteristics that are related to palmistry, we give you here some of the useful information. A basic book on astrology will give you greater insight — if you are interested:

• **Cardinal** signs (Aries, Cancer, Libra, Capricorn) have outgoing energy, comparable to a car started and building up speed.

• **Fixed** signs (Taurus, Leo, Scorpio, Aquarius) have steady energy, like a car in drive at a steady speed.

• **Mutable** signs (Gemini, Virgo, Sagittarius, Pisces) have flexible energy, like a car slowing down for a stop.

• **Earth** signs (Taurus, Virgo, Capricorn) are material-istic and are concerned with the physical body.

• **Water** signs (Cancer, Scorpio, Pisces) are medium-istic and have to do with the emotions.

- **Air** signs (Gemini, Libra, Aquarius) are intellectual and have to do with the mind.
- **Fire** signs (Aries, Leo, Sagittarius) are inspirational and have to do with the spirit.
- **Masculine** signs (Aries, Gemini, Leo, Libra, Sagittarius, Aquarius) are positive and creative.
- **Feminine** signs (Taurus, Cancer, Virgo, Scorpio, Capricorn, Pisces) are negative and receptive.

Each sign is ruled by a planet (sometimes by two planets) with its own nature and characteristics:
- **Mars** (Aries and Scorpio) — aggressiveness and male sexuality.
- **Venus** (Taurus and Libra) — beauty and the arts; female sexuality.
- **Mercury** (Gemini and Virgo) — practical mind; health.
- **Moon** (Cancer) — women, home, the personality.
- **Sun** (Leo) — self; the ego.
- **Jupiter** (Sagittarius, Pisces) — wealth, authority, professions.
- **Saturn** (Capricorn) — duty, service, restrictions.
- **Uranus** (Aquarius) — invention, genius, creativity.
- **Neptune** (Pisces) — the unconscious mind, escapism.
- **Pluto** (Scorpio) — the mass mind.

Here is a list to help you organize your thinking when it comes to relating the astrological elements to palmistry:
- **Aries** (March 21 — April 21) — Mars — Cardinal Fire — masculine. The Ram — head and brain — aggressive, headstrong, executive.

- **Taurus** (April 22 — May 21) — Venus — Fixed Earth — feminine. The Bull — throat — materialistic, beautiful, moneymaker.

- **Gemini** (May 22 — June 21) — Mercury — Mutable Air — masculine. The Twins — chest, arms, hands — practical, variable, commercial.

- **Cancer** (June 21 — July 22) — Moon — Cardinal Water — feminine. The Crab — stomach and female organs — possessive, emotional, homemaking.

- **Leo** (July 23 — August 22) — Sun — Fixed Fire — masculine. The Lion — heart, back — optimistic, self-centered, theatrical.
- **Virgo** (August 23 — September 22) — Mercury — Mutable Earth — feminine. The Virgin — digestive system — critical, subjective, serving.
- **Libra** (September 23 — October 23) — Venus — Cardinal Air — masculine. The Scales — kidneys — artistic, self-effacing, peacemaking.
- **Scorpio** (October 24 — November 22) — Mars, Pluto — Fixed Water — feminine. The Scorpion — male genitals — suspicious, sexual, engendering.
- **Sagittarius** (November 23 — December 21) — Jupiter — Mutable Fire — masculine. The Archer — liver, thighs — authoritative, athletic, professional.
- **Capricorn** (December 22 — January 20) — Saturn — Cardinal Earth — feminine. The Goat — knees, bones, teeth — ambitious, conservative, businessman.
- **Aquarius** (January 21 — February 19) — Uranus — Fixed Air — masculine. The Waterbearer — ankles, nerves — intellectual, social, inventive.
- **Pisces** (February 20 — March 21) — Neptune — Mutable Water — feminine. The Fishes — the feet — psychic, ineffectual, distributor.

Each planet is also related to a specific area of the palm and various lines that accompany it:

Mars

The inner and outer mounts of Mars; the plain of Mars, the line of Mars, and, through Aries, the head line and the cephalic line. Matters concerned with these areas thus are: sexual aggressiveness; conflict, including war and sports; competition; executive capacity; initiatory actions; activity; sensations; animal magnetism; the mind; the brain (and brain injuries and diseases); the color red (a florid hand is connected with Mars); fire and burns; courage; dentists and surgeons; barbers; firemen; mechanics; self-control; opposition.

Venus

The mount of Venus and the rays of influence that emerge from it; the girdle of Venus. Matters that are concerned with these areas and lines include: female sexuality, family, money; beauty, cosmetics; adornment; brides; beauty shops; social dancing and social clubs; interior decorating; fruits, flowers, berries; fashion; entertaining; hotels; jewelry; banks, real estate, law suits; marriage; fine arts; adultery; throat; voice; thyroid.

Mercury

The Mercury finger, the mount of Mercury, the health line, lines of affection, the practical segment (middle) of the fingers, and the medical stigmata. Matters concerned with Mercury are all practical endeavors, health matters, commerce, writing, journalism, speech, accounting, advertising, bookkeeping, clerical work, secretaries, checks, letterwriting, mail, files, teaching, short journeys, job-hunting, messengers, merchandising, news, neighbors, publishing, tennis; respiratory diseases; injuries to arms and hands; palmistry; salary; the practical aspects of marriage and children; digestive upsets; nurses; physicians; clinics; public health; the business side of living.

Moon

The mount of the moon, the line of intuition, travel lines: connected with the cephalic line through its name, The Milky Way. The moon is concerned with the abundance aspect of this line, such as waste and spending. The cephalic line often rises on the mount of the moon. Matters related to the moon and its mount are all concerns of the home, family, food preparation, and so forth that are involved with the emotional aspects of the family relationship; imagination; mediumship and intuition; the imaginative aspects of travel; catering, baking, bartending; fishing, boating, the Navy; restaurants and hotels; sleep; milk and dairies; travel agencies; conventions; the stock market; breasts and female organs (and their diseases); childbirth.

Sun

The mount of the sun, the thumb, the thumb chain, the life line, the angle of generosity; the sun also has much to do with the heart line. As such, it rules the will, the ego, all matters concerned with self and vitality; back injuries, heart disease; theatre; pleasure and children; charity; leadership; celebrities; playgrounds; sunstroke; stubbornness; wilfulness; generosity; gambling; deserts and beaches; cooperation; optimism; solariums; power; mercy, arrogance, cruelty; loyalty; kindness.

Jupiter

The index finger, the mount of Jupiter, the ring of Solomon; this planet also has much to do with the heart line, which usually rises below it; and with the health line (through its association with the liver, as the hepatic line, or the liver line). Jupiter is associated with the position in life, a good marriage and a profession; authority; wealth; wisdom; philosophy; long journeys; book publishing; travel by automobile; injuries to the thighs; liver diseases; abundance; overeating; religion; sports; large animals; justice; idealism; embassies; doctors; hospitals; extravagance; embezzlement; lawyers; financiers; hunting; philanthropy; Republican party; prosperity; speculation.

Saturn

The middle finger, the mount of Saturn, the ring of Saturn, the fate line, the bracelets. Matters concerned with Saturn are service to others, the vocations rather than the professions or business enterprises; bad luck; melancholy; scepticism; ambition; joint diseases; injuries to the knee or calf; caution; depression; fear; austerity; mountains; old age; brickwork, asphalt paving, stone; clocks, calendars, time; delays; frigidity; introspection; jealousy; drive; caves; teeth; hearing; limitations; hard work; mines; mortgages; patience; the spleen; worry; timekeepers; bone diseases; Democratic party; restrictions; obligations; fate; duty; karma.

Uranus

The ring finger, the fame line, the top (intellectual) segments of the fingers. Uranus has to do with all invention, genius, success in the creative arts, science, intellectual achievement, electricity, space travel, astrology, astronomy, mechanics, air travel and airplanes; radio, broadcasting, clairvoyance, revolution, divorce, electronics, social reform, telephone linemen, independence, freedom, innovation, physics, X-ray; injuries to ankles; nervous ailments; circulatory problems; uranium, co-ops; brotherhood; indiscretion.

Neptune

Neptune probably rules the lower mount of the moon, and thus has much to do with the travel lines that cross it and the line of intuition which arises there, particularly a reverse line of intuition; which is sometimes seen. It is also associated with the line of fame, particularly as it concerns the creative arts and inventive genius, which arises in the unconscious mind. The line of escape runs from the mount to Venus to this area, and Neptunians are known as escapists. Associated with Neptune are psychic phenomena, psychoanalysis, alcoholism, drug addiction, medicinal drugs, hospitals, hospital physicians, prisons, confinement, travel by water, creativity, mediumship, gasoline, the H bomb, utopias, seamanship, fishing, the ocean, oil, perfumes, dreams, confusion, fantasies, television and motion pictures, frauds, foot injuries, podiatrists, filling stations, floods, nudism, poisoning, smoking and the tobacco industry; retreat; yoga; the violin.

Pluto

As the so-called upper octave of Mars, Pluto probably rules the outer mount of Mars and the upper plain of Mars, the quadrangle; the lines of opposition. Pluto is concerned with the underworld, funerals, the more sordid side of sex, detectives, criminals, crime writing, taxes, reincarnation, the subconscious mind, self-control, sadism, pornography, virus diseases, steelworks, magic, witchcraft, earthquakes, guns, destruction, disorders of the prostate, regeneration; urban renewal; the police; control of pollution; pest control; insurance; legacies; boxes and containers; window shades; contracting; drugstores, druggists; chemists; trash collectors.

The more you learn about the rulership of the planets and the signs — parts of body, events, situations, jobs, places, strengths and weaknesses, diseases, love nature, and so forth — the easier it is to evaluate the hand and to assign the proper meaning to the signs you find there.

8 / PALMISTRY AND NUMEROLOGY

Each planet has a number, and things associated with the number can also be associated with the planet. To find the significant numbers of the person whose hand you are reading, start with the birthday. Each person has a personality number (the day of the month on which he was born reduced to one through nine) and a destiny number, the sum of his month, day, and year of birth.

If a person is born on the 1st, 10th, 19th, or 28th of any month, his personality number is *one*.

On the 2nd, 11th, 20th, 29th, his number is *two*.
On the 3rd, 12th, 21st, 30th, his number is *three*.
On the 4th, 13th, 22nd, 31st, his number is *four*.
On the 5th, 14th, 23rd, his number is *five*.
On the 6th, 15th, 24th, his number is *six*.
On the 7th, 16th 25th, his number is *seven*.
On the 8th, 17th, 26th, his number is *eight*.
On the 9th, 18th, 27th, his number is *nine*.

The numbers, other than the original digit, are arrived at by adding together the two digits of the birthdate to reduce it to a single digit: 1 plus 1 equals 2; for an 11th of the month birthday. And so on.

This same method of reduction is again used to get the destiny number of the individual. Take an August 6, 1946, birthday:

August — 8th month — equals 8.

6th day — gives us 6.

1946 — 1 plus 9 plus 4 plus 6 equals 20, 2 plus 0 equals 2.

1946 gives us 2.

We next add the 8 plus 6 plus 2 to get a destiny number of 16:

16 — 1 plus — gives us 7.

This individual then has a personality number of 6 (day of birth) and a destiny number of 7 (birthdate — day, month, year).

In analyzing his hand, you will look to the lines and areas of the palm relating to the planets with numbers 6 and 7 with extra knowledge and interest.

Planetary numbers:

1 Sun	6 Venus
2 Moon	7 Neptune
3 Jupiter	8 Saturn
4 Pluto	9 Mars
5 Mercury	22 and 11 Uranus

Although the Uranus numbers, 22 and 11, can be reduced to 4 and 2, respectively, these numbers are usually reserved because of their mystic quality, and because they are attributed to Uranus, the new age planet, the 11 and 22 are considered of special significance and the nature of the person is held to be completely unlike a 2 or a 4.

The planetary numbers are particularly useful in determining the destiny or profession of the individual. Here are the personality and destiny traits associated with planetary numbers:

PERSONALITY

1 — Self-centered	6 — Esthetic
2 — Emotional	7 — Escapist
3 — Expansive	8 — Restricted
4 — Explosive	9 — Aggressive
5 — Versatile	11 — Inventive

DESTINY

1 — Ego development   6 — Artistry
2 — Expression   7 — Spirituality
3 — Wealth   8 — Achievement
4 — Destruction and   9 — Adventure
      construction   11 — Reform
5 — Experience

9 / ESOTERIC PALMISTRY

Any interest in the occult sciences—palmistry, astrology, numerology, and so forth—is considered in its deeper meaning to be the beginning of spiritual enlightenment. Any occult study you engage in opens your heart to understanding. As you work in your field of knowledge, your own inner gifts begin to give to you. You start to take part actively in your own development —begin to live closely and in keeping with the cosmic Life Force. You begin to shape your own destiny in accordance with the Divine Destiny. And this is what is meant esoterically by "free will"—beginning to live in accordance with the Divine Will.

For the occultist, the hand shows not only the events of this life but the results of past and future lives as well and indicates where the subject is upon the path of spiritual achievement. Because of the wide interest in this phase of palmistry, you will need some knowledge of what is meant by the various lines and mounts of the hand in relation to spiritual development. Your own insights as they develop will help you in your understanding of esoteric palmistry.

Form

The hand is divided into three basic parts:
- *The base of the hand* (to the first horizontal line) which has to do with the life force, unconscious mind, physical body, imagination.
- *The upper palm*, which has to do with self and the self-directed life—personality, emotions, career, marriage, practical affairs.

- *The fingers,* which have to do with mind—philosophy, intellect, the way we meet the world.

The base of the hand—the physical half—includes that highly interesting member—the thumb, which has so much to do with the will aspect of our personality;
- the mount of Venus, which has to do with our love life;
- the lower mount of Mars, which governs our aggressiveness;
- the mount of the Sun—personality;
- the mount of the moon—imagination;
- the plain of Mars—the battlefield of life;
- the vital life line swoops through this area;
- and in the base of the palm the lines of fate and fame arise.

The upper part of the palm—the world—has as its lower boundary the head line, uniting the physical brain with the practical mind. The lines of fate and fame rise into this sector, and the line of health originates there, showing how our genetic make-up affects our worldly success, our personality, our way of dealing with the world. In this part of the palm lie the outer mount of Mars, the mounts of Jupiter, Saturn, Uranus, and Mercury; our heart line, our marriage and children lines, the ring of Venus (sex), of Saturn (restriction), of Solomon (enlightenment).

The upper area of the hand—the fingers—represent the higher mind and it is here we go out into the world, and the world (in the spaces between the fingers) comes into us. Each finger is related to a planet (as are the mounts below them):

- The first finger is ruled by Jupiter and has much to do with our prosperity, our good fortune.
- The middle finger (usually the longest) has to do with Saturn, destiny and limitation.
- The ring finger is allied to Uranus—marriage, fame, the arts.

• The little finger belongs to practical Mercury—here we find our skills, our children, our talents, and again, our marriage.

Somewhere in the hand every area of human activity is recorded.

The fingers themselves (and the thumb) are divided into three segments (the lower, instinct; the middle, practicality; the upper, intellect) which correspond to the three basic sections of the hand itself.

The Will

The will as it is understood esoterically is not determination, intention, aggressiveness, or "self-will." These qualities are shown by the development of the mounts of Mars and other factors. The will, as we speak of it in palmistry, and as it is indicated in the top segment of the thumb, is actually a willingness, or ability, to carry forward in one's own nature the Greater Will—to live according to the Cosmic Will, or the will of God. An understanding of this true nature of the will is needed if one is to accurately read a hand.

Understood in this way, the will is closely related to the life force, and it is understandable why the first joint of the thumb (the base) is covered by the mount of Venus (the libido, or sexual drive), and the mount of the sun (self), why it is encircled by the life line (vitality), embracing the inner mount of Mars (aggressiveness), and why the line of health and lines indicating the ability to achieve wealth traverse from this area.

We can see how the vitality and life force rise to the second joint of the thumb, which has to do with logic (reason), and then culminate in the will (top segment) —the desire to work with nature, self, the cosmos, to achieve the life purpose.

A weak top segment to the thumb shows a variable and shambling will—one who is tossed about and easily swayed by events and forces. A long and sturdy segment indicates that the person is serving his purpose in life.

In studying hands, you will soon begin to recognize from this one segment of the thumb those who are working the will of God in the world and those who are subject to the blind forces of chance. This has much to do with how the rest of the hand is interpreted.

Now a person with a weak or well-developed will segment (and any of the variations upon it) may also show a fine or too rigid or whatever form of logic (mid-section of thumb) and a firm, well-developed mount of Sun or Venus. But how these sections relate to the will section shows you how far along the individual is in his development. Esoterically, a powerful and well-developed life force (including sexuality) leads to reason (logic) and eventually to a recognition of one's role in the cosmic pattern. Those with a powerful mount of Venus and a well-developed logic and will are still using their physical nature and mentality to develop their will. Those in whom the mounts of Sun and Venus are relatively flat or smooth are using chiefly their spiritual and mental nature to develop their will. This is neither good nor bad but shows you a glimpse of a person's place upon the path.

What is important here is that the top segment of the thumb should be carefully noted and the other elements of this part of the palm—the life line, the mounts of Venus, Sun, and inner Mars—evaluated according to their degree of development. Note particularly the fullness or absence of the "Philosopher's Bump"—a bony prominence at the bottom of the thumb. Its prominence shows the person to be working with logic and reason to reach awareness rather than solely through the physical nature.

With a well-developed will sector (and always bear in mind that this shows not self-will but the desire to function according to one's destiny in the cosmic evolution), one may or may not find a strong line of destiny. A strong line of destiny is oftenest found in a generally otherwise weak hand; but it can also appear in those who are living extremely significant lives, and often will be accompanied by a strong line of fame, for these are individuals who have much to do with the cosmic evolution as it is affected by our generation.

Examine also in relation to this will factor the strength (or absence) of the line of health, the power of the life line and the bracelets (luck) and the mount of the moon.

Imagination, or the ability to draw upon the resources of the unconscious mind, opposes and also complements the power of the will as shown in the thumb. Between these areas lies the Plain of Mars—the battleground on which the armies of these two opposing forces meet and upon which they achieve peace, or union.

The fight is carried out by the inner mount of Mars (self-will and aggressiveness) and the outer mount of Mars (self-control). A large plain of Mars (it is bounded by the life line, the head line, and the line of health) is called the lucky triangle because the larger it is, the more room the forces have to move in and the less need to stand and fight. Strategy or negotiations can settle the battle without direct engagement.

A star on this triangle (battle star) can mean triumph, a hero's death, or simply quarrelsomeness (due to inner conflict), depending upon the development of the individual.

Esoterically, then, the thumb (including the lower joint, the area enclosed by the life line) represents the *Shamballah,* or Will Force, of the cosmos, complemented and opposed by the Love-Wisdom force represented by the percussion (outside of the hand) and the mount of the moon.

The bracelets on the wrist at the base of the hand are considered lucky because they represent past lives in which the conflict was successfully waged and by which the individual furthered his (or her) way to harmony with the Cosmic Will through conflict, or struggle. The life line represents the vitality of the life force in the individual during his present engagement. The mounts of Venus, Sun, and Inner Mars represent, respectively, the sexuality, personality, and self-will that propel the individual toward enlightenment but which eventually surrender to reason (logic) and after that, along with logic, to the Cosmic Will—which the individual then helps potentiate.

Love-Wisdom

The outside of the palm (opposite the thumb) is

called the percussion. It is the place where the individual meets the outside world. The lower part of the outside of the palm—in the physical, or instinctual, base section of the palm—is occupied by the mount of the moon. This has to do with the imagination but also with the part of the personality called the unconscious—the great reservoir of prehistoric memory. This has to do with the feminine, receptive, creative part of the nature.

The line of fame rises in this area of the palm and strikes upward to the Uranus finger, carrying the person with this line to achievement in the creative arts.

Across the mount of the moon run the travel lines, which represent both actual journeys (which broaden the experience and the imagination) and travels of the mind.

The head line, the lower horizontal line of hand, if it is long, runs across the upper part of this mount. Sometimes it plunges right down into the mount, indicating a highly creative and sensitive mentality.

Separating the mount of the moon from the plain of Mars is the health line (which can also indicate resources for money-making).

The mount of the moon is connected with the outer mount of Mars, which has to do with self-control and also with inner direction, and, through this mount, with the quadrangle—the area of the palm that lies between the lines of head and heart. The cosmic force of Love-Wisdom flows from the mount of the moon into the quadrangle (which lies in the area of worldly life), and it is in the quadrangle that we sometimes find the mystic cross, which indicates the working of the individual with the forces of Love-Wisdom in this lifetime—at least the ability to do so. Toward the inner palm (below the first finger) the quadrangle may be bounded by the ring of Solomon, another significator of mystic powers. The line of intuition also circles the mount of the moon, and gives its owner great intuitive powers.

The mount of the moon can also be shown to have three sectors, as do the thumb and fingers; the lowest third represents the instinctual or unconscious mind;

the middle section, the creative imagination; and the top, creative intelligence, the true Love-Wisdom. The individual develops Love-Wisdom through, first, the instinctual drives and prehistoric memories, which arise as fantasies and dreams; further developed, his imagination takes the form of creative art—poetry, music, painting, dance, and so forth; it then develops into creative intelligence, which eventually carries the individual into harmony with the cosmic mind, where he finds true inspiration and wisdom. Then, through the mystic cross in the quadrangle, he unites the lines of love and wisdom (heart and head) in his own spirit.

As the forces of will and love struggle for union on the plain of Mars, the forces of intellect and emotion struggle on the field of the quadrangle to unite in creative intelligence. The mystic cross indicates this struggle in the palm of the person who has it.

Karma

The fate line runs up the middle of the palm from the base of the palm to the base of the middle finger, or Saturn finger. To anyone familiar with the occult teachings, this line will be recognized as the indicator of karma, or past experiences to be worked out in this lifetime.

Sometimes the line of fate, or karma, is joined to the first bracelet (past lives) with a little triangle or point. This sometimes means that fate must be worked out through a physical disability or bad health brought on by the individual himself. By some it is considered a lucky sign, and usually, esoterically, a triangle is considered lucky. Actually, if the line of health intersects the fate line to create a triangle beneath the intersection, there is indication of a health crisis.

The fate line runs first through the lower part of the palm, indicating the physical body, the instinctual nature, the genetic (hereditary) problems to be experienced in this life. It crosses the head line to bring the problems into the practical, everyday life and brings them to the root of the middle finger (Saturn) which indicates service we do for others to complete our unfinished business with them. Here we meet the restrictions and limitations due to our deficiencies of development in the past. A thick mount of Saturn (this area is usually flat or depressed in comparison to the surrounding surfaces) indicates a heavy residue of duties and grievances carried over from previous lives. Our life goes out through the fingers. The Saturn (middle) finger is usually the longest. Through this finger—through service to others, work, and restrictions—we work out our debts. The segments of the finger—developed, thin, long, short—show where the individual is occupied in the path of experience, or karma.

Creativity

Along with paying our debts—filling the gaps in our life experience—we enjoy the rewards of culminated experience in past existences. This is shown in the line of fame, or fortune, which arises in the mount of the moon and rises to the Uranus finger. The great reward of past performance is being able to assist in the creation of the new—the Aquarian—age which is governed by the planet Uranus.

This finger is often associated with the creative arts—because it is so often through the arts that the meaning of a new age is expressed. Formerly this finger and the mount beneath it were attributed to Apollo (the sun) because the physical sun "veiled"—or substituted for—the planet Uranus until its rediscovery in modern times. The line of fortune is also called the line of fame because renown so often accompanies the work of an inspired creator.

The line of fortune, or fame, parallels the line of fate and moves from the instinctual area of the palm through the head line and the heart line (crossing the quadrangle) to bring past emotional experience into the practical world. Passing through the Uranus (ring) finger, the impulse of this line bears the creative force back into the cosmic creation.

Dharma

The world, and our status in it, is represented by

135

the Jupiter finger and the mount below it, upon which rises the heart line. Here the duty, dharma, of the life is worked out, the profession, the status given by marriage, wordly goods, our relation to the mores of our time, our place in the world. Esoterically, Jupiter is the training ground for the path we will choose in the world beyond—and eventually, through Jupiter, everyone experiences a profession and through it makes the choice of what area of the Divine Plan—the organization, the laws, the health, teaching, psychology, and so forth—his future energies will take. This finger is known as the pointer (and is related to Sagittarius through Jupiter as the living arrow) and points the way to the spiritual achievement, shown in this life as the worldly achievement.

Because the heart sign rises on this finger's mount, we see the worldly struggle—the endeavor of the current lifetime worked out in relation to it. The purpose of resolving the conflict between emotion and intellect that is worked out in the quadrangle flows through the heart line. Actually, it is the process of moving the emotions through the physical brain that creates the mind—the great mystery of creative intelligence. The brain is a physical organ; the emotions arise out of the physical body. It is the role the emotions play in organizing the flow of thought through the brain that produces intelligence. The heart center awakens the head center. All of this has to be worked out in the achievement part of living (the mount of Jupiter) and is carried into the cosmos through the Jupiter finger.

The mount of Jupiter is sometimes ringed with a line—clear or broken—called the ring of Solomon. This ring closes off the Jupiter mount from the rest of the worldly area—and thus shows a life dedicated to spiritual achievement, a life that is in some respect "otherworldly."

Activity

The Mercury finger has been called the "useless" little finger. What can we do with it? It can be elegantly extended or "lifted" when we hold a teacup, but even then the action is considered pretentious. Often, this little finger has more character than any other on the hand.

Mercury is the messenger, the servant of the gods. He has much to do with health and (naturally) with "lifting" (stealing), communication, talk, breathing—and all the practicalities of everyday life. He rules the practical mind.

Esoterically we must consider correspondences. The little toe (corresponding to the little finger) is almost disappearing in some ethnic groups (in some its nail has already disappeared). Can the Mercury finger function also be disappearing? It is increasingly hard to find people who want to engage in the practical occupations. This finger has much to do with marriage and children. Is the "family" on its way out?

We know the little finger functions chiefly as an aide, a helper, to the other fingers. It balances the hand. Bind it, put it in a cast, as people have sometimes to do because of accident—and one is "lost." We do need it. The line of health (and wealth) runs down the palm from the mount of Mercury (at the base of the little finger). On the percussion (the outer side of the palm) below the little finger we find the lines of affection—of marriage and children. Lines of health and health occupation appear on this finger. Its function is to be functional.

Esoterically, through this finger we use the earth and the earth uses us. Here we take, give back, and put in —and eventually (dust to dust), it is Mercury (as Hermes, god of the dead) who buries us. It is the role of the Mercury finger to utilize—to use us up, and thus return us to the land from which we came—the cosmos.

How practical are you? Mercury shows. Man is (occultly) made to be used for the purposes of the Divine. His tools crumble, his buildings crumble, his body crumbles—but he is shaped on the potting wheel, ground in the crucible; only through this experience does he survive experience.

Mercury, through the health line, gives us the vitality to do our tasks and be used up by them, to gain our income and other small possessions and to be destroyed by them, to marry and have our children and be survived by them.

Man, through the mount of Mercury, becomes the toolmaker and the doer of the business of living and then, through the Mercury finger, surrenders his physical being to the earth from which he came and carries his canniness and his talents into the machine of the cosmos.

Energy

The adventure of living is shown in the mounts of Mars. These two mounts, opposing each other but not quite, on the sides of the palm—one captured within the life line, the other lying between the lines of head and heart—are like twin buds where there might have been been other fingers but are not.

The great adventure is birth (actually conception), reflecting as it does the primal act of creation, and so the inner mount of Mars, representing the primal energy and aggressiveness, lies close to the start of the life line, between this line and the base of the thumb. Here we begin our forward march through the initiations of life—and this mount provides us with the energy to carry out our life purpose.

On the outside of the palm between the lines of head and heart lies the outer mount of Mars, the great negotiator of the peace. It represents the control we learn to exert upon our energies and how, by the twin guides of love and reason, we transform blind power into conditioned purpose.

Without the first energy, no one would dare to step out into life, much less step out into the life of the spirit which is really the great adventure. Without the second mount, the energies could not be harnessed to work the will of God. Between the two we shape our destiny.

Ego

At the inner base of the middle joint of the thumb, distinct from the mount of Venus, lies the mount of the sun. It is the place of the ego, the self—underlying the will. To understand the function of this mount, you

138

should understand that the ego is a "self-created" function of the personality. As we "grow our own body," so we create our own "self." And how many conflicts revolve around this! Many students of the occult have the mistaken notion that the ego is "bad," just because it must be dissolved before the forward step in spirituality can be taken.

Actually, occultly or pandemically, the ego must first thrive, become full, robust, like a ripe fruit, before any concept of transcending it can be entertained. Just as the full healthy body must precede the well-developed "self," so the full, expanded ego must precede the well-developed spirit. For those who have enjoyed this expansion, the transmuting of the ego into the spirit can have a reality. For those who are still fattening their ego, this should be their goal.

Painful indeed is the time of the fattening ego. We all are currently caught in the dilemma of desiring to become part of the primal mass from which the individual differentiates. We are all moving toward the goal of the communal spirit in which we merge again in a spiritual unity. Meanwhile, the self!

The transformation cannot take place without this individuation. The mount of the sun lies at the base of the thumb. We ascend from Venus (the great master, the queen of duality, and the two sexes) to the self—sun—into the pain of being an individual (of not being truly united, a two in one). Through the thumb—logic, willed reason—we rise to the dissolution of self and a willingness to work the Cosmic Will.

A well developed mount of the sun shows the fulfilling (full filling) of the self. And it is only with a full self that we can bring ourselves to deliver a genuine, complete individuality to the altar of subjection. A full self predetermines a full spirit.

With the complete fulfillment of the ego, we find freedom from the ego. Not before.

Where Are We?

When you examine a hand (your own or another's) you have to place it somewhere in the path of spiritual

139

development. For some, the hand represents the physical body. For others, it is a map of the brain. For the disciple (or even the student and for many seemingly "unawakened" souls), it is a map of the spirit. To know your place on the path and your initiations for this lifetime should be the goal of the occult student in studying the palm. The fulfilling of your spiritual destiny is your goal. And to the extent that you can work out your own purpose, you work the Cosmic Will. The picture is in your hand.

10 / HOW TO ANSWER QUESTIONS FROM THE HAND

Most of the questions that you will encounter when you read a hand will concern four general areas—love, money, health, success. But to come up with a specific answer to a question, you have to start by examining and understanding the whole hand.

Money

Money—material wealth—has much to do with the physical body, so it isn't surprising that money-making shows up in the hand. There are, of course, several ways to get money. A particular person can succeed or fail at any or all of them:

Earning It

The majority of people whose palms you read will be earning money—or expecting to earn it—through services, a job, or a profession, or through the commercial arts (journalism, musicianship, graphics, painting, and so forth). The range of potential is very great—from the most successful theatrical performer and professional man or woman down to the most menial wage-earner. To earn is *to serve*.

Making It

The money-maker is distinct from the earner in that we refer here to the person who is really in the business of making money. Manufacturing, his own business, banking, investing, real estate, speculating, selling, merchandising, and so forth, fall into this category. Making money is not only his business but his game. To make money is *to compete*.

Inheriting It

Any money received from the family—whether from an estate or legacy or as a gift—is in a sense inherited. Benefitting from an insurance policy also falls into this category. When a person asks whether he or she can expect to get some money, he or she is usually asking about an inheritance. Usually this is money that comes from the family. To inherit is *to receive*.

Marrying It

Marrying money means a little more than simply marrying a rich man or woman. Marriage can improve the position and thus the ability to make money. A good spouse can help develop talents or capabilities and is worth his or her "weight in gold." Often, of course, a husband is a woman's sole means of support. Alimony and child support and marriage settlements also come into this area. To marry money is *to barter*.

Gambling

Some people are professional gamblers—either on the market, at cards, at the races, or by making deals, or even by being a bookie. Usually those who gamble do not want to work or to be tied down to a business or tied up with a family. To make money by gambling is *to win*.

Stealing It

Money can be stolen in many ways—legally or illegally. That is, one can be a purse-snatcher, a burglar, an embezzler, a bank robber, a grafter, and so forth— all definitely engaged in the act of stealing money. Or one can be a tax evader, a stock manipulator, or otherwise legally in the business of taking money away from the government or one's fellow man. Legal or illegal, to steal is *to take*.

Saving It

Some people acquire money—sometimes quite large amounts—doing just the kinds of things you and I do but by saving part of everything they make; by being conservative in their spending; or by actually being miserly and saving every penny. This is a perfectly good and practical way of getting money. To save money is *to accumulate.*

Charity

The most obvious example of the one who lives by charity is the person on welfare. But there are a great many others who simply live by the kindness of their friends and relatives. Usually they exist on so-called "loans," which are never repaid, or by moving in and becoming a nonpaying guest. To live on charity is *to accept.*

Finding It

Anyone who discovers a rare mineral on the land, whose family grounds sprout an oil well, who comes up with a priceless antique or painting from the attic, who spots a genuine Matisse at the flea market, who stumbles over a packet of unclaimed $1,000 bills on the sidewalk, or otherwise gets an unexpected never-to-be-repeated windfall has found money. To find money is *to be blessed.*

Losing It

Although one can succeed or fail or make do by any of the above, a special talent for losing money has to be included, because it is the money characteristic of some people and their hands. The man who buys too soon or sells too late, the man who always holds a losing ticket, who always somehow misses the chance, or even actually has his pocket picked frequently, his apartment robbed, his bank fail—he is the natural-born loser. To lose money is *to evade.*

Giving It Away

There is another kind of person who gives his or her wealth away. This may be the saintly man or woman whose needs are small and dispenses what is extra to those who need it more—or the compulsive spender who can run through a month's income in an hour, or the compulsive shopper. To give money away is *to waste*.

We have italicized the key words in each of these forms of money situation because, when you have analyzed other elements in the hand, relating to wealth, you will find that these keys help you tie down to a specific marking or line what the individual will actually do about money.

The questions you are likely to be asked about money will run something like these: "Will I get an inheritance?" "Will I ever be rich?" "Will I make a killing in the market?" "Will I win the lottery?" "Will my horse come in?" "Will I sell my book? (paintings? song?)" "Will I make money on my house?" "Will I get a raise?" "Will I marry a rich man?" "Will my husband get a bonus?"

The best you can do in the way of answers is to evaluate the whole hand and individual fingers for the money potential. You have, in fact, to know the person's aptitudes and occupational potential, his general luck or unluckiness, his whole money psychology, and then pin down his sign of wealth or lack of it to a specific area. This is not easy.

We begin with the hand as a whole: The square hand always gets money by earning it, making it, but may also get money by inheritance, marriage, gambling, saving, or finding. He almost never gets it by stealing, charity, gambling—and you won't find him losing it—though he may give it away. The pointed hand almost never earns money (a man may make it), but usually it comes by gambling, inheritance, marriage, or stealing. He may lose it or give it away. The mixed hand will earn money, can make it but often won't, rarely inherits or gambles or finds, won't steal or accept charity, but often marries it. The conic hand usually marries money, often inherits it, also earns it (through a profession or the arts), can get it through charity (but this is usually an endowment or patronage of his work), may lose it or give it away. The spade-shaped hand earns money, may steal it, rarely makes it, often loses it, frequently wastes it.

Pin your person down further. If he is to make money from a profession, he needs a fine Jupiter finger; if he is to earn it in a vocation, his Saturn finger is well developed; if he is to make it in the arts, look to his Uranus finger; in practical ventures, Mercury. If his heart line starts under his index finger, and fairly high, marriage will give him position and wealth. A star on the mount of Uranus at the terminus of a strong fame line can give him wealth through creative success. For professional success, a good head line—straight and unbroken and long—is also a must; reasoning powers must be strong. The intellectual segment of the Jupiter and Saturn fingers must be firm and long. It helps if the Saturn finger leans toward Jupiter, because this brings service and position in life close together. The thumb must be well developed to give determination. Vitality must be checked because in professional life there "isn't time to be sick." The keynote to *earning money* is *to serve,* but service is not necessarily well paid; there must be a good Saturn (service) and a strong Uranus, Jupiter, and Mercury, plus an important line of fate and fortune, and influence lines radiating to the line of fortune for one to get rich by working.

Making money requires vitality and aggressiveness and a strongly physical hand—often florid, well fleshed, firm. A good line of intuition is helpful. The health line (business) will be strong. If accompanied by a cephalic line (Via Lascivia), the money is spent as fast as it is made. The mounts of Mars are firm and well fleshed; the plain of Mars is flexible but firm. Lines of influence touch many points. Often there is a battle cross. If our hero has strong lines of opposition, he may never make money. The keynote is *to compete*— and this is a key to his competition.

Inherited wealth is the strongest possibility in the

conic hand, which has much to do with ancestry and family and inherited talents. The pointed hand always wants a legacy, however. Look to the Uranus finger as well as Jupiter for an unexpected inheritance. Family position has much to do with wealth, so Jupiter is important. Look to lines of influence extending from the mount of Venus to the Jupiter finger; also to the line of fortune and to a point at the base of the palm from the first bracelet. If a line of influence extends from a family line on the mount of the moon to the line of fortune (fame), an inheritance is indicated. The key is *to receive*, so the mount of the moon should be favorable.

Marrying money is important to both men and women. If the line of the heart begins under the Jupiter finger, the marriage often improves the position. If it is starred, and a line of influence runs from the family to the mount of Jupiter, the marriage can also bring wealth. The key is *to barter;* one must have other qualities if one is to marry for money.

Gambling has to do with the line of fortune and also the line of escape. If the line of escape ties up with the line of intuition, and the bracelets, the angle of luck, and a star on the Uranus finger combine to give sudden luck, a person may be fortunate in gambling. The pointed and conic hands are our gamblers. A loser is indicated by the line of escape being frequently crossed, or broken. The health line (business) and cephalic line are also needed by the gambler. A wide angle of luck is a must. The keynote to gambling is *to win*. Often there are a well developed inner mount of Mars, no opposition lines and a poorly fleshed outer mount (self-control). The mount of the sun is strong; the will section of the thumb is long, but the logic section is full and not well firmed.

To get money by stealing as a lock-picker, one is helped by spatulate fingers. *To take,* just as to receive, is under the mount of the moon. But it is to the light-fingered Mercury—the nimble finger—that we look for the thief. The mount of the sun is also strong in thieves; as is the outer mount of Mars (Pluto). Legal stealers have a strong line of health and often a strong line of fate—and a Saturn finger that is narrow. The Mercury finger (the little finger) is often crooked. The line of escape often ties in with the cephalic line. There is often a strong fate line—and a well developed mount of Saturn. A square on the line of fate can save a thief.

Wealth through saving (accumulation) comes through Saturn and Jupiter. Often the Saturn finger leans toward the Jupiter finger. Often the whole hand cups and the fingers cling together. The individual desires wealth and can have it but is too cautious to use it. There is usually a small angle of generosity, a cramped triangle or angle of luck. The moon gives abundance but the cramped Saturn strength does not release it. Often in a saver you find small vitality, a cramped mount of Venus, and a grid under Saturn. The logic segment of the thumb is strong and there may be a stubborn thumb chain. The key is *to accumulate;* often the hand is hollow, and the fingers curve in and cling close together. The thumb is rigid and clings to the side of the palm.

Either the conic or the pointed hand is most willing to live on others—the conic out of a feeling of aristocracy and the need for time for contemplation; the pointed, because of an innate desire *to accept.* Those who need to be endowed by others often have a long, pointed will segment (tip) on the thumb, an overflexible hand, and a soft palm. The lines of family may be pronounced and the angle of generosity is often broad, indicating that though the person accepts from you, he or she would be equally generous were the situations reversed. An open angle of luck and a strong line of destiny often appear.

Found money comes on either the destiny or the fortune line in the form of a star. Often there is a strong line of intuition and other signs of spiritual attainment (ring of Solomon, mystic cross) that show the person as one who is open to *blessing.* The spatulate hand is particularly prone to this form of serendipity.

The one who *loses* money has usually a weak will segment in the thumb, a flaccid upper mount of Mars, and relatively short fingers, whatever the hand shape.

Look too for a line of escape and also for the Via Lascivia (Milky Way)—the sign of waste as well as of opulence.

The *giver* is noted for the wide angle of generosity in the higher type, usually with a wide lucky angle or triangle, and a well-shaped Jupiter finger. A favorable marking on Jupiter may indicate the desire to achieve prestige or importance through donations to others. A strong will segment to the thumb and a strong mount of the moon show a need to dominate through making others dependent. The wastrel is marked by a very flexible hand, an easily bent-back thumb, smooth fingers, and a marked Via Lascivia. The pointed, conic, and mixed hand may either lose money or give it away. The spatulate hand and the square hand usually are not bothered by this problem.

Look always at the money lines to see where they lead—to the line of fortune, fate, mount of the moon, or to the mount of the various fingers—to learn what area of spending and gaining the individual favors. To Jupiter, the position is most stable for earning or making money; to Saturn, for saving; to Uranus, for luck; to the little finger, for merchandising and stealing.

LOVE

Love appears in various forms in the palm—in its sexual form in the mount of Venus and the girdle of Venus; in its emotional form in the line of the heart; in its practical form (marriage and children) in the marriage lines, or lines of union. In the sense that marriage is destiny, the marriage M in the palm (crossed by the line of destiny and line of fortune) is the indicator.

Success in love also requires vitality—the strength of the life line and the mounts of Mars are important to it.

The **capacity** to feel love is shown in the heart line— its depth and clarity and straightness. Too straight a line, of course, can show one too direct to be romantic —it takes a bit of a curve here to allow one to enjoy sentiments and to have the flexibility needed to love wisely and well.

Romanticism in love is shown by a heart line that swoops toward the mount of the moon (imagination).

Cautiousness in love is indicated by the line's beginning under the Saturn finger.

Disappointments are shown by a fringe on the heart line.

But usually you can find a strong heart line, slightly curved, a well developed but not overly so mount of Venus, a broad swoop to a strong life line, and a reasonably fleshed mount of Mars in one who is deep and tender in the love nature.

Sexuality is shown in the mount of Venus, the girdle of Venus, the mounts of Mars, and the Via Lascivia. These pointers, with a heavy, florid and physical hand and a weak or frayed heart line, will show one who is chiefly caught up in the physical aspects of sex. With other good qualities, a firm, long thumb and long fingers and a strong heart line, the sexuality will be healthy and pleasurable. A cramped mount of Venus and a weak heart line show little sex urge.

Marriage prospects are good when the marriage lines are strong and the marriage M appears in the hand. The marriage will give happiness if the line of the heart starts under the index finger and moves strongly across the hand without breaks. Breaks in the marriage lines are the chief indication of broken marriages.

Lack of love is shown in the pale hand—the hand that is basically weak and with a thin life line and a wavery heart line. In one in whom the heart line is combined with the head line, the individual is too rational to love, although he or she may marry for convenience.

A sordid love life is shown by a broken girdle of Venus. This shows one with many sex partners—but none for long.

The questions you will be asked about love will include: "Will I get married?" "When?" "How many times?" "How many children will I have?" "Will I be happy in marriage?"

The quality of the love—and the nature of the desires—are shown in the quality of the mounts and where the heart line starts; also in the shape of the hand. The pointed hand is usually more relaxed about love, more accepting of its variables, than the other hands. The square hand shows someone who knows what he or she wants—and it usually is a good marriage with children. The conic hand is likely to be romantic about love and may have a broken girdle of Venus, because the heart rules the head. The spatulate hand is practical about love—often two or more marriages are indicated. The mixed hand is usually a generalized person, and often has a variety of love indicators and they often contradict each other.

HEALTH

Health questions that arise are usually put to you by someone who has a problem: "How long will I live?" "Will I have to have an operation?" "Will my arthritis get better?" Remember that you are not a diagnostician and don't try to give medical advice. Health indications are, however, very noticeable in the hand and learning how to handle them is one of your tasks, because discretion (to avoid the possibility of suggestion) is needed.

A physician can see indications of many health problems in the hand—and so will you as you become familiar with the many symptoms that appear. You will, however, report them with care. The general ailments of the human body appear clearly in the hand:

Accidents

These are of course a frequent cause of death and can also be serious and confining without being fatal. Look for them in breaks in the life line. There is, however, a kind of hand that is prone to accidents—often fatal—and also to brain accident, or stroke. This is the fully fleshed, florid hand, often with strong mounts of Mars and Venus, and with a short, deep life line. There is often a battle cross—and lines of opposition may also appear. This is a naturally aggressive person with much drive who will often also drive his car too fast and work too hard and will also be engaged in dangerous sports. There is little you can do except warn the person of particular danger at the time of life when the accident or accidents will be of greatest risk.

Heart Attacks

A red dot on the life line often indicates a heart attack at the time of life shown on the line by the dot. Impending circulatory problems can be seen in a pale hand, especially one with pale fingernails.

Tension

This is so commonly seen in the hand that we even have a designation—the nervous hand. A fretwork of tiny lines all over the hand, much fraying and fringing of the lines of head and heart, often a chained or fringed life line, show the threat of tension to the individual.

Mental Illness

This is shown by breaks (sometimes overlapped) in the head line. Sometimes the line forks or splits. Sometimes a head line that dips deeply into the mount of the moon (heel of the hand) and ends with a tassel or which frays at this point shows mental deterioration. White dots on the fingernails also indicate a nervous-system disorder.

Emotional Illness

This can be seen in the line of the heart—islands, breaks, chains, splits, especially when this is also a "nervous" hand.

Hospitalization

Serious illness that puts you into a hospital can be seen in an island on the life line. A near-fatal illness may be indicated by a star on this line—the only place where a star is considered unfavorable.

There are many other indicators—a chain at the start of the life line shows a sickly childhood; extremely dry skin and fragile fingernails, thyroid disorder; islands, dots, circles, grids, and crosses on an area of the palm related to a particular organ of the body may also show the danger of weakness in that organ.

The inner mount of Mars and the head line have to do with the brain and also with accidents; the mount of Jupiter and the liver line (health line) have to do with the liver; the mount of the moon controls illnesses of the stomach and female sex organs; the heart line and the mount of the sun, the heart; the Uranus mount has much to do with nervous disorders; Mercury, with general health and also with respiratory diseases. The outer mount of Mars shows problems of the male genitals; the mount of Venus, throat and thyroid disorders; the Saturn finger bone and joint diseases.

Important to observe in connection with any health problem are such things as a double line or a square (both protective), whether the line continues after the break, or island. If so, recovery is indicated.

The health line itself is important in all this. Absence of the line is said to be salutary. Breaks, crosses, islands on it can indicate illness. The line is best for health and good fortune if it does not intersect either the head or life line. The point at which the health line intersects the life line is believed to indicate the time of death—even if the life line continues. It is never wise to tell the person the age at which he or she is likely to die.

SUCCESS

Those who ask about success may either be referring to their everyday life, their career, their social success, their marriage—but oftenest you are asked the question by someone in the arts, including the theatre, because these people depend more upon public acclaim for financial reward.

Success in the normal way of life is shown in the index finger and the mount below it and in the destiny line. A good Jupiter gives a good position in life. Success in the arts is shown in the Uranus (ring finger) area. A firm line of fortune culminating in a star gives fame—and success. It is wise, when discussing success or its lack, to point out how the person is perhaps hindering himself—by weak will (thumb), lines of opposition, or by stubbornness (thumb chain). It is very easy to point out the possibilities of success and good fortune in a hand. It is more difficult to explain how and why the success will be hard to achieve. Saturn, the restrictive finger, often indicates a fate that interferes with the person's achieving a heart's desire.

11 / HOW TO USE THE LANGUAGE OF PALMISTRY:

An Alphabetical Guide to Basic Terms

Apollo Finger: Apollo, god of the sun, had much to do with the arts, vitality, and health. He is the symbol of male beauty. His twin sister is the moon goddess Diana. In palmistry and astrology, the sun represents the individuality, self; the moon represents the emotional (personality) side of the nature. Ideally, the moon (feelings) should be ruled by the ego (sun). Then there will be harmony within the person. The ring finger (now designated the Uranus finger) was formerly called the Apollo, or sun, finger; the cushion below it was termed the mount of Apollo, and the line of fame (or fortune), the line of Apollo. A well-developed mount of Apollo and especially one with stars or triangles, along with a well-formed Apollo finger, indicates one whose ego is mastering his emotions and who is expressing the "form" side of life through the arts or profession rather than through moods and physical experience. When a palmist says, "You have a well-developed Apollo," a cultivated, esthetic nature or use of talents is indicated. "You are neglecting Apollo," means that you are not paying enough attention to the esthetic side of living.

Affection Lines: The lines of affection, commonly called the lines of marriage or of union, lie on the outside of the palm just below the little finger. They are horizontal lines, sometimes intersected by vertical lines (blessings) that indicate children. Sometimes the intersecting lines indicate a break in the relationship.

This depends on whether they stop at or cross through the lines of affection. Although a deeply marked line of affection is a marriage indicator, the term "affection" is often applied because the union is not always a legal arrangement.

Angle of Generosity: This refers to the angle formed by the extended thumb and the side of the palm and the index finger. The wider it is, the more open-handed and generous is the individual. A cramped angle of generosity shows a careful, if not stingy, person.

Angle of Luck: The angle of luck is the angle formed by the line of the head as it separates from the life line. The wider the angle, the luckier the person. If a line of health appears on the hand, it completes a triangle with the other two lines and this is called the lucky (or great) triangle.

Bar: This is usually a small horizontal line on a mount or plain of the palm or a cushion of the thumb or finger. A bar, unless it is crossed by a vertical line, is considered unfortunate. When so crossed, it forms a "cross," and is still considered an obstacle but a way out is promised. In general, horizontal lines indicate problems; vertical lines are constructive.

Basic Lines: These are the major lines of the palm—the life line, the head line, and the heart line. The first two appear on every palm; in some palms the head line and heart line are combined, and there is only the life line and one basic (or major) horizontal line on the palm.

Battle Cross: The cross of battle appears in the mid-palm in the triangle formed by the head line and life line and the line of health. It often is formed by a horizontal line combined with the line of fate. It indicates a struggle in life—a strongly aggressive, or even quarrel-some, individual. It may also indicate one who dies in battle—usually a hero's death. To engage successfully in many present-day enterprises, a battle cross is necessary.

Bracelets: These circles of luck are not on the palm itself but ring the wrist at the base of the palm. Bracelets, especially if unbroken, are considered lucky. Sometimes they are used as measure of length of life—one bracelet for each 25 years. If the top bracelet rises to the middle of the palm in a point, it indicates either an inheritance or that the individual is his own worst enemy healthwise.

Branch: When a line continuing in its own direction sends a secondary shoot off elsewhere, this is called a branch. In the lines of head or heart, it indicates a new direction at the point of time where it takes place. A branch of the life line often runs all the way around the base of the thumb. This indicates vitality in old age. But a branch in the life line can also indicate an accident or illness after which the life is not the same. A branched heart line can indicate a change of personality—or an emotional illness that "divides" the individuality, depending on the direction of the branch and the strength of the individual line.

Brilliance Line: The line of brilliance is another name for the line of fame or fortune or the sun (Apollo line). It is particularly worthy of being called the line of brilliance when it culminates in a star. If the line of fame (fortune) is doubled, the sister line is often so designated because it increases the genius accompanying such a phenomenon.

Break: When a line stops completely or stops and then continues with or without an overlap, it is considered a break and indicates a crisis in the area of life the line governs. Many breaks in a line indicate an unfortunate situation for matters concerning that line; many breaks in the girdle of Venus, for example, show many love affairs or a sordid form of sexuality.

Business Line: This line is synonymous with the line of health, or the hepatic line. Apparently, a sound business sense can be equated with a sound constitution. Men who are "money-makers" often have a strong line of business, or health.

Cephalic Line: This is a term for the second or outer of two lines that occur when the health line is doubled. Cephalic means skull, and this line is a key to both the hard-headed businessman who uses business as an outlet for his drive and vitality, and the businessman who is also a big-time spender. The line is also called the Via Lascivia—the wanton way—so, with other indications, its possessor may be wasteful both of cash and sexual energies. Another term for this interesting and productive line is the Milky Way—again indicating abundance, extravagance, prodigality.

Chain: A chain or a chained line is comprised of a series of circles or islands linked together to look like what it is called—a chain. It shows weakness, or sometimes overemphasis, in what the line governs. A chained start to the life line shows the usual childhood illnesses; a chained head line shows anxieties; a chained heart line, emotional problems. Most important of the chained lines is the thumb chain, which runs down the thumb at its second (middle) joint, between the mount of the sun and the logic segment of the thumb. A thumb chain shows an argumentative disposition—a person hung up between will and logic.

Chance Lines: These are random lines that appear in various places on the palm and have their own specific indications for the mount on which they appear or other lines that they connect. Generally, vertical lines are considered constructive; horizontal lines, destructive.

Circle: A circle on the palm is just that—a circular formation—and can appear on a line or free-floating on an area of the palm. Usually it is an indication of re-striction or confinement. On a line, the circle is usually considered an island and is unfortunate; a series of circles on a line creates a chain.

Clubbed Thumb: Heavy, thick thumb, bent back, to take the shape of a club. Shows an indomitable, stub-born will.

Color: The color of the palm and of the skin of the hand is taken into consideration when the hand is read. A yellowish cast is saturnine in nature and restrictive to vitality; a palish cast shows lack of vital energy; a pink palm is considered wholesome; a reddish palm, an over-ly aggressive nature; a bluish palm or skin or fingernail shows diminishing vitality. The color of dots or other marking, including the color of the lines, is read in the same context.

Conic Hand: This is one of the five basic hand types (eight really, if you consider the elemental, philosophi-cal, and nervous hand) and is the one least often seen. It tapers toward the fingers, and the fingers are also tapered (tubular) and the hand has an unmistakable rounded shape. It shows a creative and imaginative mind and is found in many professional people—par-ticularly those who lean toward the theoretical and idealistic side of their calling.

Cross: Two intersected lines—one vertical, one hori-zontal—form the cross, and it may appear on any area of the palm and also may be formed by intersections of the major lines with secondary and minor lines and so forth. When formed with a specific line, it has to do with events of that line; when free standing, like the battle cross or mystic cross, it means a struggle in the area of the palm to which it relates. The vertical of the two lines is constructive; if the stronger, it shows the battle will be won; the horizontal is considered destruc-tive (or unfortunate); if the stronger, it may show that the battle will be lost. Two major crosses appear on the palm—the battle cross, in the angle or triangle, between the head and the life line, indicating a fighter; and the mystic cross, which appears in the quadrangle between the head and heart lines and which shows the individual struggling for spiritual achievement. Both appear on the plain of Mars. The battle cross indicates the struggle between the ego and the emotions; the upper, mystic cross, shows the struggle between the physical forces and those of the spirit.

Cushion: This is an elevation on the inside of the finger-tip— and it may be thick, soft, peaked, round, and so forth—or a pad on the inside of the fingers or even a mount at the base of the fingers or the thumb or on the heel of the hand. The development, or lack of development, of these cushions is studied in the evaluation of the palm.

Depth: This term is used in connection with the lines and indicates how effective the specific line may be. Depth gives strength and importance to a line and the matters the line rules. In the basic lines—head, heart, and life lines—depth is an important quality.

Destiny Line: This term is ordinarily applied to the fate line (Saturn line) which runs from the base of the palm to the middle or Saturn finger. But it is sometimes also applied to the lines of fame, health, and influence. These are considered destiny lines because they show how the world affects you. In other words, what comes from the outside is beyond the individual's control.

Dot: A dot, usually red on the palm, white on the fingernail, but possibly black, yellow, or blue, shows an existing health problem. A white dot on the finger-nail indicates a nervous disorder, a red dot on the life line may warn of a heart attack; a blue dot, of a cir-culatory block off; a yellow dot, of a bilious condition.

Double Line: Any line on the palm may be doubled for part or all of its length. A double line gives protection and also strength to the line it accompanies. The extra line sometimes has its own name—the sister line to the life line is called the line of Mars; a sister line to the line of health, the cephalic line, and so on. A double line is always considered significant.

Elemental Hand: This is one of the basic hand types and belongs to the primitive (or sometimes mentally retarded) person. Chances are, you will not see it, but in case you do, learn to recognize it in advance and avoid reading it. Fingers and thumb are short and poorly developed; there are few lines on the palm. Often head and heart line are combined. The palm and fingers are usually thick and clumsy. Some brutish people in civilized life have this hand.

Escape Line: The line of escape runs across the bottom of the palm from the mount of Venus to the lower mount of the moon and thus can cross the life line if it is long. It shows the person who runs away from problems into fantasies (sometimes into drink, drugs, over-eating) or otherwise escapes confrontation with his real nature. Crossing the life line, it may mean escape via suicide; touching the fame line, escape by artistic creation.

Fame Line: The line of fame is synonymous with the line of fortune and the line of Apollo (sun). It runs vertically up the palm from the outer sector (mount of the moon—imagination) to the base of the Uranus (ring) finger (success). This line does not always appear in the hand; when it does, fame and celebrity are destined.

Family Lines: The lines of family are the third (and usually the faintest) of the series of lines that curve within the life line. That is, we have a line of life; some-times it is doubled (line of Mars); sometimes a line of family appears as a fainter third line (or series) within this area. Family lines show early or late family influence, and often lines of influence that radiate from the mount of Venus to the rest of the palm are connected with these family lines, showing family influence.

Fate Line: The line of fate is called, as well, the line of destiny and the line of Saturn. It begins in the middle at the base of the palm and runs up the palm to below the middle finger (Saturn). It may be absent. Present, it may be strong and distinct or wavering and broken. The line of fate shows what control life has over you (as distinct from the control you exert over your own destiny). It is tied up with what the occultists call karma, the duties you have brought over from past lives. It may bring good fortune as well as bad—but it shows one who is ruled by events beyond his or her control rather than one who makes his own luck.

Fingers: The fingers are studied for their length, shape, straightness, knottiness or smoothness of joints, firmness of the tips and fullness or slimness of the phalanxes (segments between joints). The fingertips are particularly important in indicating the basic shape of the hand—and even the nails are related to the character and destiny of the individual. The fingers are also related to the mount at their base. The index finger, or pointer, has the attributes of the planet Jupiter—position in life, authority; the middle finger is related to Saturn—service and vocation; the ring finger (Uranus), to the arts and to success; the little finger, Mercury, to the practical endeavors. The first (lowest) phalanx of each finger relates to the instinctual element; the middle, to the practical or worldly element; the top phalanx, to the intellectual part of the personality.

Firmness: The firmness or flabbiness of the various areas of the hand—the palm itself, the various mounts, such as that at the base of the thumb and the one at the heel of the hand, and those at the base of the fingers—are evaluated to understand the approach of the individual to the areas of life related to the mount. Firmness is also considered in the handclasp and in the flexibility or firmness of the thumb—or the hand as a whole—when bent.

Flexibility: Both the hand itself and the thumb and the individual fingers are bent and moved to test their flexibility. A rigid hand, thumb, or finger indicates a stiff, unyielding nature; an overly flexible hand, thumb, or fingers shows one too easily swayed. Normal flexibility is considered an asset.

Fork: A fork can occur at the beginning or ending of a line; in this instance the line splits into two parts which usually are of equal strength or weakness. A fork is not bad if the line continues strongly as a double line, but a fork, like a break in a line, indicates a crisis. It is usually considered unfortunate if at the end of a line, in that the matter terminates in a crisis and a split. At the beginning, it means trouble at the start or two influences at work that eventually consolidate and therefore harmonize. If the line continues strong, the fork is not destructive. A fork differs from a branch in that two lines of about equal strength emerge. In a branch, an offshoot line goes elsewhere while the main line continues.

Fortune Line: This is another name for the line of fame (also called line of Apollo, line of the sun, and line of brilliance). It has to do with the public acclaim that comes from achievement and has much to do with success in the arts. It runs from the base of the palm, usually starting on the heel of the palm (mount of the moon) outside the fate line, to the base of the ring finger (Uranus finger).

Frayed Line: A line is called frayed when it is badly broken. This usually indicates disorder or even dissolution in matters ruled by the line.

Fringed Line: This is a line that has many little lines running down from it (sometimes up as well). The line

of the heart is often "fringed," indicating many disappointments in love if the lines run down; upward,
many occasions for heart interests.

Generosity: This is shown by the angle of generosity—
the spread of the thumb away from the inside of the
palm and index finger. The wider the spread, the more
generous the nature.

Great Triangle: In the middle of the palm, in the plain
of Mars, a triangle is formed by the lines of head and
life with the health line as a base. The larger this triangle is, the better for luck. It is particularly good if
the line of health does not touch either the line of life
or line of head. This area is also called the lucky
triangle.

Grid: This is a crosshatching of horizontal and vertical
lines (also called a grille) and may appear anywhere on
the palm. It means problems—but problems that are
open to solving.

Grille: Another term for the crosshatching—or grid—
described above.

Girdle of Venus: This is a semicircular line, often
broken, sometimes incomplete, that begins between the
index and middle fingers and loops below the middle
finger to the space between the ring and little fingers.
It denotes sexuality—a firm, clear line shows a wholesome but perhaps overemphasized physical love life;
a broken, chained, or crosshatched line indicates a
number of trivial affairs, a sordid love nature.

Hammer Thumb: This is an unmistakable thumb (once
seen), with a thickened back-bent tip that looks like a
hammer. It is considered the sign of an extremely materialistic nature with an indomitable will. I have,
however, seen some possessors of such a thumb who
have bent their will into a determination to overcome
their materialistic nature.

Hand: In palmistry, the lines on the palm are read, but the shape of the hand as a whole, with fingers and thumb, has a great bearing on the reading. The hands are grouped as square, spade-shaped, conic, pointed, and mixed—but there are other classifications, including the elemental, the philosopher's hand, or knotty hand, and the nervous hand. The type of hand has much to do with the mental and emotional traits of the person and the profession toward which he or she will be directed. Color, size, smoothness, strength, warmth— all these are considered in evaluating the hand. Both hands are read. In a right-handed person, the left is considered subjective and occult, the hand the person is born with; the right is objective—what one does with one's life (or has done) and the worldly side of life. The opposite is assumed in a left-handed person.

Head Line: The head line is one of the three major lines of the hand and is the lower of the two basic horizontal lines. It starts on the inside of the palm above the thumb and above, or joined to, the start of the life line. It divides the lower instinctual nature of the palm from the upper or practical-world section. The head line has to do with the physical brain as well as the intellectual development. Its strength, depth, and direction as well as its length show the mental capacities of its owner.

Heart Line: The heart line is the upper of the two (usually) major horizontal lines on the palm. It shows the qualities of the feelings as well as the love nature and emotional strength of the individual. It starts below the index finger or below the space between the middle and index finger and sometimes below the middle finger. Sometimes it runs up into the space between these fingers. It swoops across the hand, straight or curved, sometimes runs all the way to the outside of the palm. Sometimes it dips down or up. Sometimes this line is missing; if so, head and heart lines are combined and indications of both intellectual and emotional nature must be read from the one line.

Health Line: This is also called the line of business, the hepatic line, the line of Mercury. It runs diagonally across the palm from the base of the thumb to below the little finger. It forms the base of the lucky triangle made up of the lines of head and life and health. The line of health is often missing—and this is a sign of good health. This line has much to do with business success, money-making, as well as with physical endurance. In fact, its presence often indicates that health will be injured by too much effort in business achievement.

Hepatic Line: This is the health line described above. It is so called because the liver ("hepatic" is derived from the Greek word for liver) was once considered the seat of health (or illness), as to a large extent it is. The health line is also termed the liver line.

Horizontal Lines: The two major horizontal lines in the hand are the lines of heart and head. So far as chance lines (those that appear at random or related to other lines) are concerned, horizontal lines are considered obstructive, vertical lines facilitating.

Inside of Hand: The palm is the inside of the hand. In referring to the inside of the palm itself, the area above the thumb is meant; the outside of the palm is the side opposite the thumb, and is called the percussion.

Influence Lines: These are lines that originate in the mount of Venus at the base of the thumb and radiate out across the life line, showing people, events, situations that influence the life of the subject. Where these lines are directed—to the various mounts or triangles or the quadrangle—and where they cross major lines—life, fate, fame, health—events of importance occur. These lines are studied for both the character of the event and for the timing of such occasions as marriage, accidents, access of fame, problems, and so forth.

Inner Mount of Mars: There are two mounts of Mars.

One is on the inside of the palm above the start of the thumb and within the life line. This is called the inner or lower mount of Mars and has to do with the aggressiveness and energy of the subject. The outer (upper) mount of Mars lies on the outside of the palm below the heart line and has to do with self-control.

Intuition Line: This is a curved line (also called the line of the moon) which starts at the outer base of the palm on the mount of the moon and curves upward toward the outside of the hand below the little finger. It may cross the health line in its progress. Often missing, this line, when present, shows a person with great intuitive sense and understanding. It is sometimes reversed, running along the rim of the percussion (outside of the palm).

Island: This is a circular or oval area in a line, alone or in series, that shows a crisis of some kind from which the person will recover. It is considered both critical and unfortunate.

Joints: The joints of fingers and thumbs are studied in the evaluation of the hand for their smoothness or knottiness. The first joints of the fingers are the knuckles. On the palm they are fronted with the mounts, or cushions, that relate to the finger. The second joint is the middle joint—it separates the instinctive and practical segments of the fingers. The third joint is the top joint, relating the practical and intellectual segments of the fingers. On the thumb, the lower (first) joint is at the base of the hand, covered by the mount of Venus. The middle (second) joint of the thumb lies at the place where it separates from the palm, and the top (third) joint separates the middle (logic) segment from the tip (will) segment. Smooth joints show passivity; knotty joints show struggle.

Jupiter Finger: Jupiter is known as the king of the gods, master of law and philosophy, and the planet Jupiter in astrology has much to do with one's position in life. He rules the sign Sagittarius, the arrow pointed at the heavens. In palmistry, the index finger is the Jupiter finger, and this finger and the mount at its base also indicate position, general well-being, and optimism. The line of the heart often originates below this finger. Like the arrow of Sagittarius, this finger is "the pointer."

Knuckles: The knuckles are the first joints of the fingers and underlie the mounts of Jupiter (index finger), Saturn (middle finger), Uranus (ring finger), and Mercury (little finger). The knuckles are seen on the back of the hand and may be smooth or knotted like other joints.

Knotty Hands: Hands with knotty joints are considered to be the hands of the thinker, the philosopher, whereas the smooth-jointed person is considerably more emotional and less a reasoner. The knottiness of the joints must be considered separately on each finger, because smooth and knotty joints can appear on the same finger.

Lean: This refers to the slant of the fingers toward each other. A finger that leans toward its neighbor shows an interdependency of affairs of one finger upon another.

Left Hand: In a right-handed person, the left hand is considered the hand you were given by fate while the right hand is considered to reveal what you have done with your life. The left hand is usually read first and then the right. The two hands may be quite different.

Length: Length of fingers and thumb is given in relation to each other as well as to the palm. The fingers are considered long if the longest (usually the middle finger) is as long as the palm. A thumb is considered long if it reaches (when laid against the side of the palm) to the middle joint of the index finger. Length of the individual segments (or phalanges) of the fingers and thumb are also compared, as is the length of the fingernail (the bed of the nail, not the overgrowth). Length usually indicates development; extra-long fingers or long segments can show overdevelopment; just as extra short fingers or phalanges can show underdevelopment.

Life Line: This is one of the three major lines of the hand and has to do with life force and vitality as well as length of life. It starts on the inside of the palm and swoops down the hand toward the base and sometimes curls around the thumb.

Lines: The lines are the tracings on the palm of the hands. The major lines are the lines of life, head, and heart; secondary lines: lines of fate, fame, health; minor lines: lines of affection, girdle of Venus, travel lines, bracelets. The lines also include special markings— crosses, grids, circles, squares, triangles—and many other little lines that radiate from various areas of the hand, indicating influence, travel, money, family. Lines may be doubled and then the sister line has its own designation. The complete list of lines (see individual description) includes: lines of life, head, and heart; line of fate (also called line of Saturn or line of destiny); line of fortune (also called line of Uranus, line of Apollo, and line of brilliance); health line (also called the hepatic line, the liver line, line of business, and Mercury line); cephalic line (also called Via Lascivia and Milky Way; a sister line to the health line; line of Mars, a sister line to the life line; line of intuition, a crescent-shaped line on the outer base of the palm (also called line of the moon and line of Luna); lines of affection also called marriage lines); family lines (lines within the life line and paralleling it); influence lines, lines that radiate from the base of the thumb; ring of Solomon, ring of Saturn, girdle of Venus, which loop below the index, middle, and ring fingers; line of escape, a horizontal line at the base of the palm; line of opposition, on the outer side of the palm below the marriage lines. There are also lines of travel and of reputation, and various other markings, such as crosses and squares, and the bracelets (or rascettes) which circle the wrist below the palm. It is the study of these lines in relation to their depth, strength, special markings, placement, and direction that comprises palmistry.

Liver Line: This is another term for the line of health—also called the hepatic line, and the line of Mercury. It has to do with health, business, and success in money-making.

Lower Mount of Mars: This is the inner mount of Mars, called lower because it has to do with the lower, aggressive drives—as opposed to the upper, or outer, mount of Mars which has to do with control and direction of these drives. The lower mount is on the inside of the palm above the thumb and within the life line.

Luck Line: The line of luck is also known as the fame line, the fortune line, the Apollo line, the line of the sun, the line of brilliance. It starts at the heel of the hand and runs up to the base of the Uranus finger. One who has this line strong and clear is destined to good fortune.

Lucky Angle: This is the angle formed by the lines of life and head. When it is wide, it gives good luck to its possessor. When it is narrow, it narrows the luck.

Lucky Triangle: This is the great triangle formed by the lines of head and life and the line of health. The greater the area of this triangle, the luckier the life.

Luna: This is another name for the moon, and we find it used in such terms as mount of Luna (mount of the moon); line of Luna (line of intuition or line of the moon). The mount of Luna (moon) covers the outer base or heel of the palm. The line of Luna (line of intuition) is a crescent-shaped line beginning on the base of the palm and circling up toward the outside of the palm below the little finger.

Magic M: This letter is called the sign of marriage, money, and mysticism. It is sometimes found in the palm, roughly formed by the lines of life, head, and heart, cross-barred by the line of fate or sometimes by both the line of fate and line of fame. The general type of the hand must be evaluated to understand what the M stands for—oftenest it stands for marriage in the hand of a woman (two crossbars mean two marriages), money in the hand of a man, and a mystic purpose if accompanied by the mystic cross and ring of Solomon.

Markings: These are small marks that appear in various places on the palm. Fortunate markings are the square, triangle, star (except on the life line); they also include a series of horizontal lines. Unfortunate are the cross, circle, island, a series of horizontal lines, a grid (or grille). In a line itself there may be islands, chains, forks, fringes, tassels, and overlaps of breaks that also are considered unfortunate. Some special markings are the battle cross and the mystic cross and the magic M.

Marriage Lines: These are also known as lines of union and line of affection. They lie on the percussion, the outside of the hand below the little finger (Mercury). Deep, clear lines indicate a marriage; shallower lines indicate attachments that may not be legally sanctified or at any rate do not result in marriage. If these lines are intersected by vertical lines, the vertical lines signify children; if a line crosses a union line, it signifies a break in the relationship.

Mars: Mars was the God of war and represents in both palmistry and astrology the natural aggressiveness of the individual. On the palm we find an inner and outer (also called respectively lower and upper) mount of Mars, a plain of Mars, and a line of Mars. The inner mount of Mars (also called lower) is on the inside of the palm above the thumb and below the life line; it represents the instinctual, aggressive drive; the outer (upper) mount of Mars lies on the outside of the palm between the lines of heart and head or between the mounts of Mercury (below the little finger) and the moon (heel of the hand). The plain of Mars is the mid-palm (or hollow of the hand). It includes the lucky angle formed by the lines of life and head or the lucky triangle, when the line of health is present, and the quadrangle. The battle cross (if present) appears on the plain of Mars. The line of Mars is the sister line in a double life line and increases vitality.

170

Medical Stigmata: Apparently those who are destined for a career in the health field are marked with the medical stigmata. This is a series of vertical lines on the mount below the little finger (the Mercury finger). Other parts of the chart indicate what aspect of the health field the person will enter. But his destiny is clear.

Mercury: Mercury is known as the messenger of the gods and is concerned in astrology and palmistry with the practical mind and everyday occupations—writing, short trips, speech, handiwork, and also with medicine and health. The little finger is the Mercury finger, and the mount of Mercury, which has much to do with health, commerce, and practicality, lies below it. The line of health or business (also called the Mercury line) runs to this mount. The lines of affection (marriage) and children lie below this finger on the side of the palm below this finger. When we speak of a well-developed Mercury, we indicate a lively, practical, common-sense approach to life. A series of vertical lines under the Mercury finger show one who can be occupied in the health field successfully.

Milky Way: This is another name for the cephalic line (also called the Via Lascivia), which is a sister line to the health line. It improves wealth and business sense and also indicates extravagance.

Mixed Hand: Of the five basic types of hand—square, pointed, conic, spatulate, and mixed—the last is a hand that is made up of various elements of the other four and cannot be classified as basically one or another type. Yet it takes on a distinct appearance as a type in itself. Because of the prevalence of the mixed hand in the United States, each finger and the hand as a whole must be studied to interpret it correctly. It is the hand of versatility—teachers, researchers, journalists have this hand.

Money Lines: The money lines are usually lines of influence that radiate out from the mount of Venus to connect with various other destiny lines in the hand. The sister line of the health line is often known as a money line because it indicates prodigality and waste.

Moon: The moon has much to do with the emotional life—and is allied to women and children, the home, the imagination, intuition, change, the unconscious mind. In palmistry, the mount of the moon lies on the heel of the hand. From it arises the line of fame. It sometimes is marked with the line of intuition (also called the line of the moon or line of Luna). Sometimes the head line or the heart line curves down into this mount. Travel lines radiate from it. It is sometimes referred to as Luna, after the old name for the moon, and a well-developed Luna (or moon) indicates great imaginative quality.

Mounts: The mounts are the cushions or pads that may be well or poorly developed on the palm below the fingers. They are named, like the fingers, after the planets. Below the index finger we have the mount of Jupiter, indicating position in life; below the middle finger, the mount of Saturn (rarely present), indicating melancholy; below the ring finger, the mount of Uranus, indicating success in the arts; below the little finger, the mount of Mercury, which has to do with health and practical living. The mounts of Mars are two—one lying on the inside of the palm, above the thumb, but below the start of the life line; the other on the outside of the palm, between the heart and head lines. The inner mount of Mars has to do with aggressive drive; the outer with self-control. The mount of the moon (imagination) lies over the heel of the hand. The mount of Venus (sexuality) is enclosed by the life line and overlies the base of the thumb. The mount of the sun lies over the middle joint of the thumb and has to do with self (ego). The mounts are landmarks of the palm. Lines are directed toward these mounts, showing in what direction one's aptitudes lie. The development of the mounts (or lack of it) and the firmness or the flabbiness of the mount reveal the development and the nature of the individual in relation to matters or traits the mount governs.

Mystic Cross: This cross, which shows spiritual development and sometimes a psychic gift, lies in the quadrangle—the area between the heart and head lines. It is evaluated in connection with the line of intuition and the ring of Solomon.

Nails: The nails are examined in reading the hand in order to help in evaluating the hand type and also to understand extra things about the character and personality of the subject. Usually a nail follows in shape the finger shape—pointed, square, spade-shaped, conic (oval); or else the nails, like the fingers, can be mixed. The nails may also be unusually long, broad, slim, short in relation to the rest of the hand. Sometimes white dots appear on the nails—these can indicate nervous problems. The color of the nails—pale, pink, yellowish, bluish—is evaluated for the vitality of the individual.

Nervous Hand: A hand that is interlaced with numerous lines—almost to seem etched by them—is known as the nervous hand because so much nervous energy flows through these minor and chance lines of the hand. The hand can be of any shape but is commonly a mixed or a conic or a spatulate hand. The Uranus finger basically rules the nervous system. A nervous hand is really a new-age hand. Although it can be analyzed like any other hand, the amount of tension in it always governs the delineation.

Opposition Lines: These lines run horizontally from the outside of the hand onto the palm across the outer mount of Mars and may intersect or cut across the health line or the lines of fame and fate. As this is the mount that has to do with control of aggressiveness, the lines denote control by opposition. They threaten the affairs involved in the lines they cut across.

Palm: The palm is the inside of the hand between the fingers and the wrist, including the base of the thumb. The length of the palm is used as a gauge to determine whether fingers are long, medium, or short. The size, shape, firmness, fullness, or flatness of the plam are evaluated in understanding the nature of the subject. In the study of palmistry, the palm includes the mounts of the planets and also all the major and most of the minor lines that are examined. The major artery of the palm runs up the hand under the mount of Venus (the base of the thumb), and there is said to be a psychic center in the middle of the palm which becomes awakened if the reader stares at it or gently caresses it with thumb or finger.

Palmistry: Palmistry is the study of the lines and other markings on the palm in relation to certain areas of the palm, called mounts, and the plain of Mars and the triangle or lucky angle. The study of the hand as a whole in character-reading is more properly called hand-reading or chiromancy—but today palmistry is the term used to embrace the reading of the entire hand.

Percussion: This refers to the outer edge of the palm between the wrist and the little finger. The word actually means "to strike" and this is the striking edge of the hand (as differentiated from the slapping area, the palm). Either the head or heart line or both can run across the hand into the percussion. The lines of marriage (affection) appear on the percussion; the opposition lines originate here. The outer mount of Mars and the mount of the moon cover the percussion.

Phalanges: These are the segments of the fingers and thumb and are attributed to certain characteristics. The first phalange (above the palm) on the fingers has to do with instinctual drives, the second with practicality; the third with intellect. On the thumb, the first phalange is covered by the mount of Venus (libido) and the mount of the sun (ego); the second has to do with logic; and the top phalange with will. The length and the thickness or slimness of the phalanges are taken into consideration as well as their comparative length.

Philosopher's Hand: This is a knotty hand (knotty knuckles) and is often a large and tapered hand. Often there is a large knobby protrusion at the base of the thumb below the mount of Venus. This hand is often considered as a sixth basic hand type (seventh, if you include the elemental) in addition to the conic, pointed, square, spade-shaped, and mixed hands.

Pointed Hand: This hand may be small or large, but it is often small and has smooth knuckles and small almond-shaped nails. It is, ethnically, the Mediterranean hand and the Oriental hand. It is the hand of beauty, the arts, the cosmetic world and sometimes indicates a psychic or mediumistic nature. Sometimes a pointed finger appears on a mixed hand, but in the pointed hand all fingers are pointed.

Plain of Mars: This is the middle of the palm, and along the borders of this plain the mounts rise. If depressed, this plain is called the hollow of the hand. If very hollow, it shows insecurity and fear; if very elevated, over-aggression; if fairly level, a reasonably equitable nature. The plain embraces the lucky triangle or angle of luck (between the life and head lines, with the health line making the triangle) and the quadrangle, which lies between the lines of head and heart. The battle cross appears within the angle or in the triangle. The mystic cross is found in the quadrangle, which represents an area where the emotions and intellect are balanced.

Quadrangle: This area is the upper plain of Mars and lies between the lines of head and heart. On the outer side of the palm the quadrangle runs into the outer mount of Mars; on the inside of the palm it runs into the mount of Jupiter (below the index finger). In the lower plain of Mars (the triangle between the lines of head, life, and health), the life forces are brought under the control of the intellect. In the quadrangle, the emotional forces are brought under the control of the intellect. The mystic cross is found in the quadrangle.

Rascettes: These are lines that circle the wrists below the base of the palm and are commonly called bracelets. Bracelets are considered lucky, especially if unbroken, and the larger the number, the greater the luck. If the top bracelet rises to a point at the base of the palm, it is said by some to be fortunate, by others to mean that one does himself harm.

Rays of Influence: This is another term for the lines of influence that rise from the mount of Venus and radiate out into the plain of Mars, bringing influences to bear on the lines they contact—life line, line of fame, fortune, or health. They are lines, but are called rays simply because they radiate (or fan out) from this sector.

Reading: Reading is used in connection with palm-reading, card-reading, tea-leaf reading, an astrological, numerological, or even a psychic reading, because of the belief that one's whole life—past, present, and future—(as well as past and future lives) is recorded in the psychic archives of the ages. Thus the reference to the Recording Angel. When a person reads your palm, he or she is actually reading your life record from the keys given in the hand.

Reputation Lines: These are a series of vertical lines on the mount of Uranus, which are favorable for success and general esteem. Crosshatched, they lead to notoriety rather than fame.

Right Hand: In a right-handed person, the right hand is considered the record of what one is doing with the fate he was handed at birth. The left hand is the hand that records one's fate as it was given. Thus, the left hand, the subjective hand, is read first; then the right, the objective hand, is compared to see how you have worked out or used the gifts you were given.

Ring of Saturn: This is a line, clear or broken, that begins between the index and middle finger and circles the base of the middle finger to the space between it and the ring finger. As the line of fate rises to this area, and the Saturn finger represents fate and delays, the ring denotes restrictions—sometimes severe limitations in profession, poverty, excess carefulness. As you know, the actual planet Saturn is famous for its rings—which occultly are said to be the nursery of monads who failed in their first rounds on earth and after confinement in Saturn will have to return again as part of the mineral kingdom on earth and work their way up through the vegetable, animal, and human kingdoms to spirituality.

Ring of Solomon: This ring is named for King Solomon, who is said to have had a magic ring that enabled him to converse with animals and birds. The ring of Solomon gives mystic tendencies, psychic abilities, and an interest in the occult. It begins between the index and middle fingers and swoops around to the inner edge of the palm. Look for the mystic cross and the line of intuition in interpreting this ring, which may be clear or broken.

Saturn Finger: In myth, Saturn represents time. In astrology, restriction, limitation. In occult teaching, limitation. In palmistry, we find Saturn giving its name to the middle finger, the mount (if any) beneath it, and sometimes to the line of fate, which is also called the line of Saturn. It also appears in the ring of Saturn, a halfcircle line that loops below the middle finger and brings limitations. The Saturn finger (middle finger) represents service, duty, vocation, restrictions. The mount of Saturn, if developed, indicates melancholy, a depressed attitude, self-harm. Usually this area is flat, but it can be fat. The line of Saturn (fate line) suggests restrictions by the outside world, but it can also indicate a fated vocation, hard work, and in its best aspects brings success and achievement.

Set of Thumb: This refers to the angle the thumb makes with the palm of the hand and also with its flexibility and whether it is set low on the side of the palm or is more elevated. A well-set, like a well-proportioned, thumb is considered a great asset to the character.

Shape: The shape of the hand is considered one of the

important first clues to the character. Hand shapes are actually seven, but usually there are only five considered: the pointed, conical, square, spade-shaped (spatulate), and mixed. The elemental hand (seen only in primitive people or the retarded), the knotty hand, or philosopher's hand, and the nervous hand are also considered. The shape of the hand also indicates professional bent: square—the worker, the doer, practical occupation or business; pointed—the arts, beauty, esthetic matters; the coneshaped—teaching, law, creative artists; spade-shaped—inventor, mechanical genius, science, engineering; mixed hand—journalists, teachers, researchers, scientists; philosopher's hand—creative thinking. The shape of the fingers often corresponds to the shape of the hand, as is often true of the shape of the fingernails. The shape of the thumb is particularly relevant to the character.

Signs: This is another term for special marks that may appear anywhere on the palm or on a line. Fortunate signs are the square, triangle, star, and a series of vertical lines; unfortunate signs are the cross, the grid (crosshatch), a series of horizontal lines, circle, island, chain, fringe, or fork.

Sister Line: This is a line, usually lighter but not necessarily so, that doubles a major or minor line on the palm. These usually reinforce the effect of the line, strengthen it, and also give protection in the areas the line pertains to. Sometimes these lines have their own special names. The sister line of the life line is called the line of Mars; the sister line of the health line, the cephalic line (or the Via Lascivia, or Milky Way). The sister line of the fame line is called the line of brilliance.

Size: Size of the hand—and also the relative size of the palm, the thumb, the segments (phalanges) of the fingers, the nails, the angle between the thumb and index finger when the hand is spread (angle of generosity), the quadrangle (the area between the heart and head lines), and the triangle (formed by the life line, head line, and line of health)—are all important in evaluating the character and life. Although the size of the hand is relative to the size of the person, it soon becomes clear who has little hands and who has big hands in proportion to the figure as a whole.

Secondary Lines: These are lines that may or may not appear on the hand but are important when they do. The basic lines are those of life, head, and heart. The secondary lines are those of fate, fame, fortune. Minor lines include the line of intuition, family lines, lines of influence, lines of opposition, marriage lines, the rings of Solomon and Saturn, the Girdle of Venus, and the various grids, series, crosses, and other markings that make up the network of the palm.

Separations: The space between the fingers, like any clinging or slant of the fingers toward each other, is significant. The space shows the world entering the life and psyche of the subject. A generous space allows outside events to affect you and also permits one to separate the various departments of life in a way that is wholesome. The examination of spaces between the fingers is in many ways as important as the fingers themselves.

Series: Sometimes small lines appear in a series of two, three, or four on a mount or other area of the palm or on the inner part of the phalanges of the fingers. Horizontal lines are considered worrisome and represent problems; vertical lines are generally considered fortunate and constructive. In a series, the lines are emphasized for good or bad. When a series of vertical and a series of horizontal lines overlap, they form a grid and are considered an obstacle to be overcome.

Slant: This refers to the tendency of some fingers to lean together or to slant toward each other when the hand is relaxed. Any slant of a finger toward another shows a bringing of the area ruled by the leaning finger into the orbit or influence of the finger toward which it slants or upon which it seems to depend.

Solomon's Ring: This is a curved line, named for King Solomon, that swings down from the space between the middle and index fingers to the edge of the palm below the index finger. It is said to give mystic powers.

Solar Line: This is the fame line, also called line of the sun, line of Apollo, and the line of Uranus. It gives "a place in the sun" to its lucky owner—and was derived from the word Sol, or sun. This name was given to the fame line because this line rises to the base of the finger that was earlier called the Apollo, or sun finger, and is now attributed to the planet Uranus.

Spade-shaped: This is applied to one of the five basic hand shapes—the hand of the inventor or mechanical genius—which is wider at the top than at the base and the finger tips of which are broad and often thick—and very useful. The spade-shaped hand (also called the spatulate hand) usually has nails that are broader at the top than at the base. On the mixed hand, it is often the middle finger that is spade-shaped, or spatular.

Spatulate: Spade-shaped—broader at the tip than at the base of a finger; broader at the top than at the base when used to describe a hand. The typical fingernail is broader at the top than at the base. A spatulate hand or spatulate fingers show mechanical aptitude, inventiveness.

Split: A dividing of a line into two parts, each continuing. Shows a crisis and a complete change in the line that is affected.

Spread: The spread of the hand and the spread of the thumb are taken into consideration when evaluating the character. If the hand, when stretched, has a wide spread it shows a person with a widely embracing mind and personality—someone who is open-minded and versatile in abilities. A narrower spread shows someone more limited, with a cramped outlook, narrow relationships and a closed mind. The spread of the thumb away from the inside of the palm gives the angle of generosity. The wider the spread, the more generous the person.

Square: This is one of the free-floating markings that may appear anywhere on a palm or on a line. It is considered protective and in general fortunate.

Square Hand: This is one of the basic hand shapes. Palm is square in shape; fingers may be long or short, but are in any case blunt and square at the tips, with square fingernails. This is the competent hand; the hand of the doer.

Star: This is usually a fortunate marking (do not confuse it with the cross, which is made up of a vertical and horizontal line crossing each other.) The star must have five or more points. The star usually indicates achievement. When it appears on a mount, it gives great prowess in the area indicated. The star is unfortunate only when it appears on the life line. There it can indicate self-sacrifice.

Sun: The ring finger, the mount below it, and the line rising to this mount (fame line) were originally attributed to the sun. Since more has been learned about the planet Uranus, it has seemed more appropriate to credit this rulership of this grouping to the planet of genius, Uranus. This is particularly so since the fame line is often involved with luck and has been called the line of luck. Now attributed to the sun is the mount just below the middle joint of the thumb above the mount of Venus. This mount has to do with the self, the ego—the overcoming of the physical and emotional sides of the nature by self-identity.

Tassel: This describes what appears when a line terminates (or begins) in a lot of little wavy lines that look just like a tassel. It is considered an unfortunate end (or beginning) for the affairs of that line—dissolution.

Thickness: This is one of the gauges for the character of the hand, the fingers, the areas of the palm, including the mounts and the middle of the palm, and particularly the tip of the thumb. Thickness and firmness in the mounts indicate strength; in the tip of the thumb, strong will; in the center of the palm, heaviness and aggressiveness; in the fingers and in the hand itself, it shows heavy-handedness and often clumsiness.

Thumb: The thumb is related to the will—particularly the top segment—and as the mount of the sun lies beneath it, it can be taken to be ruled by the sun and to represent the individuality. The fairly long, reasonably firm thumb is one of the best indications of firm character and responsible ego. The angle of generosity is seen by stretching the thumb away from the palm and gauging the angle it makes with the side of the palm.

Thumb Chain: A chained line that descends from the place where the thumb joins the palm across the middle joint, it shows a stubborn and willful personality.

Time: Time is judged on a line of the palm by segmenting it according to the average lifespan (if the line is of average length) and extending the time if a long life is indicated. Sometimes it must be judged according to infancy, childhood, youth, maturity, and age. But with skill, a reader can pin down an event to within a few years.

Tip: The tip of a finger or the thumb, the top phalanx, are useful in determining the hand type. The lines on the balls on the inside of the tip (where we press to have our fingerprints taken) can be seen only with a magnifying glass, but the kind of tips that come to little cones indicate a great deal of intellect as well as competence. Flat, smooth tips show more theory and less application of intellect.

Travel Lines: These lines arise on the mount of the moon and cross into the plane of Mars, sometimes intersecting the lines of fate and fame and even the life line. Only important journeys are shown by the travel lines, though many lines indicate frequent travel.

Triple Line: Just as a line can be doubled, it can be tripled. This is less common than a double line but it reinforces even more the strength of the line.

Triangle: Small triangles on a mount or other area of the palm or on a line are considered fortunate. If the line of fate or fame culminates in a triangle, it improves luck. But there also are areas of the palm called triangles. The most important of these is the great or lucky triangle, which is formed by the lines of life, head, and health and which occupies the lower plain of Mars in the middle of the palm. If the triangle is large, it is fortunate; if smaller, it cramps the luck. It is luckiest if the line of health does not touch either the life or the head line. Whenever major or secondary lines form a triangle, this is considered to reinforce the prowess of the subject in the areas touched by the sides of the triangle. A small triangle at the base of the palm has been called fortunate for money, dangerous for health.

Union: Lines of union are also called lines of marriage or lines of affection. They appear on the outside of the palm below the little finger and run over onto the mount of Mercury.

Upper Mars: This is an expression used for the outer mount of Mars, indicating that it represents the higher nature of the aggressive drives. It lies on the side of the palm between the lines of heart and head above the mount of the moon.

Uranus Finger: Uranus in myth represents the heavens. In astrology it represents genius, the unexpected, modern technology, and rules the Aquarian Age. A Uranus transit is important in bringing about marriage. In palmistry it rules the ring finger, the mount below it, and the line of fame which rises to this mount. Creative genius, whether in arts or science, is shown in this finger, its mount, its line. It represents fulfillment.

Venus: Venus is the goddess of love and beauty. In astrology, she is considered a benefic planet, bringing good to the affairs she contacts. In palmistry, the mount of Venus, representing the love nature, is at the base of the thumb, encircled by the life line. The lines of influence radiate out from this mount. The girdle of Venus, revealing the nature of the sex life, is a semi-circular line running from between the index and middle fingers to the space between the ring and little fingers. Clear, it represents a strong but wholesome sex life; broken, many affairs.

Vertical Lines: Lines running vertically are believed to be fortunate; lines running horizontally are destructive. The line of fate and the line of fame both are vertical; the line of life also swings down the hand. A series of vertical lines on any of the mounts or phalanges or on the plain of Mars usually indicates help for problems that worry the subject.

Vitality Line: Lines that accompany—double or triple —the life line; the double of the life line is also called the line of Mars.

Waver: When a line, instead of being straight and clear, wavers and has uncertain direction, the strength of the line is weakened.

Width: The width of the hand, the width of the finger tips, and of the nails are considered in judging the character of the hand. Width is especially important in the mount of Venus (if too cramped, it cuts the love nature) and in the spread of the lucky triangle (formed by the head line, life line, and health line), the lucky angle (formed of head and life lines, without the health line), and the angle of generosity—the spread of the thumb away from the hand.

Worry Lines: These are chance lines, vertical and horizontal, that characterize the nervous hand. They show a temperament much involved in the tensions of everyday life. These small lines often form around the line of head, the line of heart, the life line, and anything in the hand must be judged in relation to the nervous tension that governs much of the subject's destiny.

12 / TWO SAMPLE HANDS AND THEIR READINGS

You get to know hands by looking at hands—and no illustration can take the place of a hand you actually hold and study. This is because lines have a tendency to rise and fade away according to the mental set of the person at a particular time. Still, the basic lines remain clear and can be studied.

We show on the following pages some sample hands, beginning with a simple one, and proceeding to greater complexity, to demonstrate to you how complicated a palm may be—and for you to see a full reading from start to finish. In one of the readings, both the right and the left hand of the pair are shown and read.

SAMPLE HAND A

This spatulate hand shows someone with a great deal of competence and ability as well as the power of creative thought. It is, however, rather relaxed and flexible, and the thumb has a wide spread, indicating generosity but some lack of determination. The lines themselves are interesting. The life line is not very sturdy but it is protected by a strong line of Mars (doubled life line) which greatly improves the chances of a normal life span. The line of health is also strong (almost as strong as the life line) and does not touch the life line, which is good. Both the lines of head and heart are long

SAMPLE HAND A

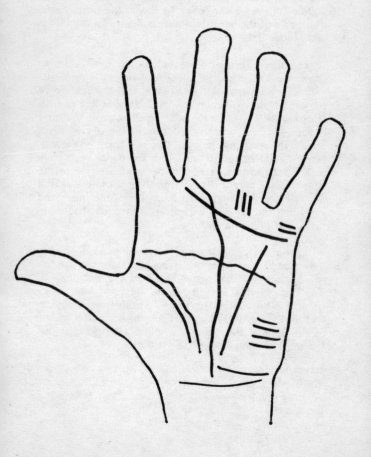

and curved. The head line begins separately from the life line, showing an adventurous nature; it curves away from the heart line to the mount of the moon, indicating some creative thinking and not too much domination by logic. The wavers in the line show that the person, a woman by the way, is not overly dominated by thinking, though there is good mental power. This is borne out by the heart line, starting between the index and middle fingers—a tendency to throw the heart away. The curve of the heart line also indicates an emotional and tender nature.

The three vertical lines below the Uranus finger show one who could be successful in the arts, music, painting, but perhaps the most interesting feature of the hand is the extremely long and devious line of fate. It makes its way from the wrist itself to cross the lines of head and heart and to rise far to the side of the Saturn finger. Interestingly enough, this is a hand of a Sagittarian—and there is no one like a Sagittarian to bravely seek his (or in this case, her) destiny—aspiring to the stars. We see here a person who lives her life in search of what she was meant to be, giving generously and garnering the rewards and disappointments that eventually add up to having *lived*.

Two marriages—or deep relationships at least—are indicated. Travel lines are strong, indicating a number of trips abroad that strongly affect the imagination. The luck of this person should be good—the lucky triangle is broad and the line of health does not intersect the life line. One bracelet runs high into the middle of the base of the palm. An inheritance may be due but may be hard to realize.

SAMPLE HAND B

These remarkable hands show how different a pair of hands can be. They are the large and beautiful conical hands of a large and well-proportioned man. Confronted with hands as variously marked as these, where does one begin? First, with the shape and texture of the hand itself. The conic hand is often the hand of the well-born and the professional—and in this case the hand is that of a lawyer and educator of good family and position. The long tubular fingers are smooth and show fine co-ordination of the various faculties. Mounts are moderately developed, except for the mounts of the moon and Venus, which are well developed and firm. The thumb shows a certain amount of caution by its shape and good logic by the long and waisted middle section. The top section (on the left hand) shows a somewhat weaker will but this is better developed in the right hand (how one has lived). A thumb chain shows a certain amount of stubbornness. The hand itself is rather pale and shows a threat of circulatory problems at some point in life.

In the left hand, the life line is firm and of a length to show a normal life span. There is an indication of threats to life, accidents in the 20- to 30-year period. A fork from the fate line runs around the base of the thumb showing an active old age. The head line here is very interesting. It starts separately from the life line, showing a tendency to adventurousness but it is separated (left hand) into four sections or doublings, indicating a diversity of possibilities in the line of thought of this person. Note that it is firmed and united in the right hand. This is not uncommon among Virgos (this palm belongs to a Virgo)—the head line has been vastly improved by education and put upon a single track. In the right hand it runs down into the mount of the moon indicating a great creative use of the mental faculties. This person has actually *four* professions and is successful at all of them! In other words, the four mental bents indicated in the left hand have

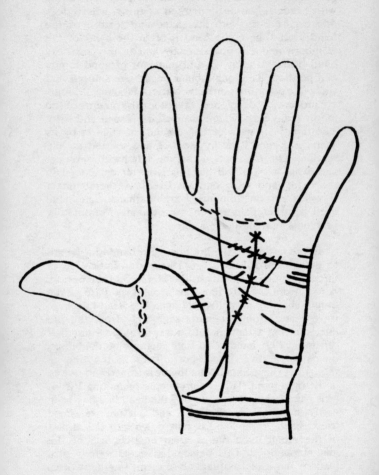

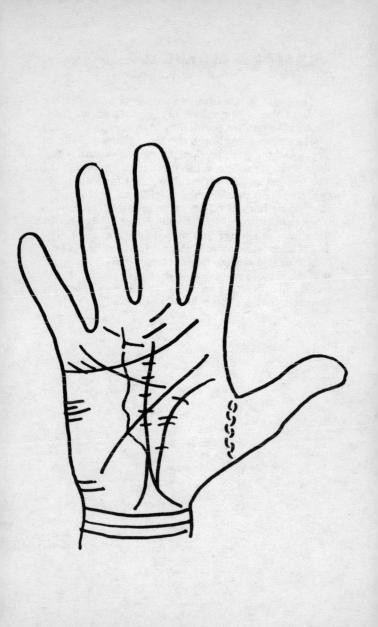

been unified into a single fine intellectual development that has still resulted in four professions.

The heart line is firm and strong, beginning in the left hand almost at the base of the index finger, showing improvement of position by marriage. It has many breaks and crosses, borne out by the strong girdle of Venus and the well developed mount of Venus, which show someone active in the joys of the physical body. The fate line in the left hand is strong (many mutable sign people—Virgo, Gemini, Sagittarius, and Pisces—have strong lines of fate because they tend, more than other signs, to bend to the will of destiny) but in the right hand is shorter and with many cross lines. The line of fame takes off in both lines from the line of fate, indicating that destiny leads to fame. In the right hand, this line is more wavery than in the left. Lines of both travel and opposition are strong in both hands, and the bracelets indicate both good health and good luck